Philipp M. Becker

Investing in Microfinance

GABLER RESEARCH

Philipp M. Becker

Investing in Microfinance

Integrating New Asset Classes into an Asset Allocation Framework Applying Scenario Methodology

GABLER

RESEARCH

Bibliographic information published by the Deutsche Nationalbibliothek
The Deutsche Nationalbibliothek lists this publication in the Deutsche Nationalbibliografie; detailed bibliographic data are available in the Internet at http://dnb.d-nb.de.

Doctoral thesis, University of St. Gallen, Switzerland, 2010

1st Edition 2010

Editorial Office: Ute Wrasmann | Sabine Schöller

Gabler Verlag is a brand of Springer Fachmedien.
Springer Fachmedien is part of Springer Science+Business Media.
www.gabler.de

Cover design: KünkelLopka Medienentwicklung, Heidelberg
Printed on acid-free paper
Printed in Germany

ISBN 978-3-8349-2567-1

Acknowledgements

An idea that merits examination is a sine qua non for a doctoral thesis. My studies at the University of St.Gallen and the inspiring atmosphere in the Asset Allocation & Research department of LGT Capital Management provided me with the roots and wings to pursue academic merits. In particular, I am very grateful for having met Professor Pascal Gantenbein, who inspired me at the very beginning of my academic career and supported my academic development until the very end. Hence, first and foremost, my deepest gratitude is to Professor Pascal Gantenbein. I also would like to thank Professor Andreas Grüner for co-supervising this study and providing thoughtful comments and suggestions.

Furthermore, I am also greatly indebted to Dr. Magnus Pirovino Walter Pfaff and Dr. Alex Durrer from LGT Capital Management. They create an open platform for the thoughts of their employees and give advice as well as support whenever needed for new ideas. One of these ideas – the integration of scenario methodology in asset allocation – fascinated all of us. Their guidance, enthusiasm and the financial support enabled this project.

Moreover, I am very grateful to all scenario workshop participants for their essential contributions. Firstly, Professor Minx, Dr. Frank Ruff and Dr. Burkhard Järisch from Daimler AG, who contributed extensive scenario analysis know-how. Secondly, with Damian von Stauffenberg, Patrik Huber and Dr. Annette Krauss three highly regarded microfinance specialists donated some of their valuable time to give me and all other workshop participants an insight into microfinance. Thirdly, many more colleagues of LGT Capital Management spent time to create microfinance scenarios – Johannes Oehri, Hanspeter Oehri, Dr. Matthias Feiler, Mark Rall, Dr. Marie Mikl, Michael Simmeth, Oliver Karius and Wolfgang Hafenmayer. Their input in the scenario workshops are a principal component of my thesis.

Finally, many close friends and my family supported me during the inspiring but sometimes difficult times of writing this thesis. Their contribution is invaluable.

Wädenswil, May 2010 Philipp M. Becker

Brief Contents

Table of Contents

Abstract

An important task in asset allocation is the generation of forward-looking input parameter estimates for the portfolio optimization. Quantitative models allow an analysis of the past – dependent on data availability. However, even a long data history creates a backward-looking indicator. To overcome these limitations this study implements also a qualitative forward-looking approach and applies it in a comparative assessment. The scenario methodology is introduced as an analysis tool for asset allocation input parameter estimates. Besides a theoretical process outline, this approach and a quantitative assessment are performed for microfinance investments. A detailed description of the scenario process using the example of microfinance with a number of workshops and participating experts for scenario analysis, microfinance, asset allocation and emerging markets is outlined. The outcomes of the scenario analysis are several scenarios for microfinance including input parameter estimates for a portfolio optimization. As a result, the asset allocation model with qualitative input parameters reveals the attractiveness of microfinance debt investments for risk-averse private investors. In contrast, the quantitatively generated input parameters result in inappropriate portfolios with very high microfinance debt exposure. Recommendations for microfinance investments for different investor categories are provided and the relevance of a qualitative, structured scenario process for asset allocation is highlighted.

Zusammenfassung

Ein wichtiger Beitrag zur Asset Allokation ist die Schätzung von zukunftsgerichteten Parametern zur Portfoliooptimierung. Quantitative, von der Datenverfügbarkeit abhängige Modelle ermöglichen eine Analyse der Vergangenheit. Daher führt selbst eine lange Datenhistorie nur zur Entwicklung von vergangenheitsbasierten Indikatoren. Angesichts dieser Limitierung implementiert die Studie auch einen qualitativen, zukunftsgerichteten Ansatz. Dabei wird die Szenarioanalyse als ein Instrument zur Schätzung von Parametern für die Asset Allokation vorgestellt. Neben einer theoretischen Prozessdarlegung wird der Ansatz am Beispiel Mikrofinanz durchgeführt und eine Ableitung von quantitativen Parametern vorgenommen. Eine detaillierte Beschreibung der Szenarioanalyse Mikrofinanz mit mehreren Workshops unter Mitwirkung von ausgewiesenen Experten aus den Bereichen Mikrofinanz, Asset Allokation und Emerging Markets wird dargelegt. Das Ergebnis der Szenarioanalyse sind verschiedene Zukunftsszenarien für Mikrofinanz, welche auch Schätzungen für Asset Allokation Parameter enthalten. Die Integration der Ergebnisse in eine Portfoliooptimierung zeigt die Attraktivität von Mikrofinanzinvestitionen für risikoaverse Privatinvestoren auf. Im Gegensatz dazu führt eine ausschliesslich quantitative Analyse zu einem extrem hohen Mikrofinanzexposure. Abschliessend werden Portfolios für verschiedene Investorenkategorien optimiert und die Relevanz einer strukturierten Szenarioanalyse in der Asset Allokation hervorgehoben.

List of Figures

List of Abbreviations

Cat bonds	Catastrophe bonds
CDO	Collateralized debt obligation
CLO	Collateralized loan obligation
DFI	Development finance institution
DMF	Dexia Microcredit Fund
EFSE	European Fund for Southeast Europe
EM	Emerging markets
FX	Foreign exchange
IFC	International Finance Corporation
KfW	Kreditanstalt für Wiederaufbau
LGT CM	LGT Capital Management
MF	Microfinance
MFI	Microfinance institution
MIV	Microfinance investment vehicle
MPT	Modern portfolio theory
NAV	Net asset value
NGO	Non-governmental organization
PAR30	Portfolio at risk with payments more than 30 days in default
SPV	Special purpose vehicle

rAGMF responsAbility Global Microfinance Fund

USD US Dollar

1 Introduction

1.1 General motivation

In recent decades in finance and particularly in asset allocation quantitative methods gained considerably in importance. This trend is fostered by the rising processing power of computers. The impact of those quantitative approaches on investment decisions is controversial. Irrespective of numerous exceptionally successful applications for example in portfolio theory, misleading quantitative models also inspired the securitization of debt obligations and the underestimation of risks. The blind reliance on quantitative models has turned out to be inadequate.

Quantitative tools can only be as smart as the input. Even a perfect quantitative model depends on the input variables. Furthermore, the models are often also calibrated with these data. As a result, the expression "garbage in, garbage out" is common in finance. Additionally, a smart model has to be developed. Again, negligent underlying assumptions and econometric imperfections create problems. An example for both is the mortgage backed securities market (MBS) and the securitization of these papers in collateral debt obligation (CDO) structures. Firstly, the securitization of MBS included diversification estimates that did not prove of value. If the housing market in California deteriorates, all house prices fall and diversification is mainly not applicable. Secondly, many investors analysed a short period to generate risk and return estimates in addition to rating agencies' seal of approval. However, a quantitative assessment of a short period does not give an appropriate indication of risks. In many cases, a change of the situation or the macroeconomic framework for instance rejects the prior analysis. In conclusion, the abilities of quantitative methodologies must be implemented advisedly.

The emergence of a new asset class is a challenge for asset managers. On the one hand generally first movers receive an additional risk premium. On the other hand an assessment of an emerging asset class without several years of history is complex. The enrichment of asset allocation by catastrophe bonds (cat bonds) at the end of the 1990s was such a case.[1] Kielholz and Durrer (1997) claimed that investments in cat bonds improve the risk-return pattern of an investment portfolio. From today's perspective a clever investment, but for asset managers the assessment of return, risk and correlation estimates proved to be problematic. A potential underestimation of risk often results as tail risks cannot be observed in short time periods. Such an event also affected cat bonds in 2009. According to some special purpose vehicle structures (SPVs), the counterparty risk of big insurance companies was taken into consideration by investors leading to a sharp decline in this illiquid asset class. As a consequence, quantitative assessments of short term periods of an asset class for asset allocation purposes are inappropriate.

Scenario methodologies are a qualitative approach to address this issue. In absence of historic data over a longer period, the modelling of potential futures is a key element to derive estimates. Furthermore, these estimates are forward-looking and can include innovation or mission drifts of a problem set. Obviously, emerging asset classes are subject to innovation and changes such as regulation or investment guidelines. In addition, scenario planning fits into the regime thinking of asset allocation. Moreover, it allows a quantification of specific parameters in the developed scenarios. In conclusion, a scenario process might be an adequate tool in cases where quantitative assessments are inopportune. Looking into the future is very useful at the beginning of any decision making process including investment decisions.

The idea for introducing a scenario analysis approach into asset allocation came up with the following problem. Microfinance is a currently emerging asset class with similarities to cat bonds. The analysis of return expectations and underlying risks is complex. Furthermore, there is only little experience regarding investments in this sector and the objects' characteristics change continuously. As mentioned, in such an environment quantitative analysis tools are limited. For this reason, a qualitative methodology such as scenario analysis comes to the fore.

[1] Catastrophe bonds – debt instrument mainly issued by insurance companies to distribute the risks of natural disasters.

1.2 Research questions

The main objective of this work is to examine the appropriateness of quantitative and especially qualitative methods to integrate new asset classes into an asset allocation framework. Additionally, the study gives a detailed introduction into microfinance – a new asset class – and assesses the attractiveness of this asset class in an asset allocation framework focusing not only on quantitative methods but also on qualitative methods. Therefore, two main research areas develop. First, an assessment of quantitative and qualitative methods to integrate new asset classes into an asset allocation framework applies. Secondly, both methodologies are illustrated with microfinance representing a new asset class.

Research topic 1: Integration of new asset classes into asset allocation

Research question 1.1: Are quantitative methods a comprehensive approach to integrate new asset classes into an asset allocation framework?

Research question 1.2: Are qualitative methods such as scenario analysis a comprehensive approach to integrate new asset classes into an asset allocation framework?

Research topic 2: Microfinance in an asset allocation context

Research question 2.1: Is microfinance an attractive asset class in an asset allocation framework based on quantitative methods?

Research question 2.2: Is microfinance an attractive asset class based on the qualitative method scenario analysis?

1.3 Outline

Research question 1 is discussed complementary with research question 2. Firstly, chapter 2 gives an introduction to asset allocation based on μ / σ-optimization and the shortfall concept. Furthermore, a categorization of investor types is outlined. Thereafter, chapter 3 provides an overview of scenario methodologies. Moreover, the approach of combining asset allocation and scenario analysis is described. Thirdly, a detailed insight into microfinance is provided in chapter 4. Besides the idea of microfinance, a market overview and the current market conditions are described. Furthermore, an assessment of selected microfinance investment vehicles is conducted and the problems of a common quantitative integration into asset allocation are discussed. Fourthly, a detailed description of a core element of this study is outlined. Chapter 5 describes the scenario analysis microfinance executed by a comprehensive pool of experts during 2009. This process generates qualitative information about microfinance scenarios and also enables deriving quantified asset allocation input parameters. Fifthly, in chapter 6 the input parameters from the scenario process as well as from the quantitative index analysis are integrated into an asset allocation framework. Finally, chapter 7 concludes this study referring to the research question and explicitly describes implications for asset allocation practitioners.

2 Asset Allocation Framework

2.1 Asset allocation

Asset allocation is the decision process of allocating a portfolio to several considered asset classes. Furthermore, it also labels the resulting weighting. Hence, asset allocation is a decision-making process leading to a customised portfolio.[2]

The investors' preferences are a key element in an asset allocation process. These preferences can be modelled in an investors' utility function. However, the exact determination of a utility function for an investor is complex. Thus, the parameters return, risk and liquidity are often used as a reasonable proxy.

Three essential criteria for financial investments are return, risk and liquidity. Firstly, an investment should return a reasonable profit. Secondly, risks associated with the investment process and the investment itself shall be limited or at least offer an attractive relation to return expectations. Finally, an investment shall be liquid, which means marketable at any time without high transaction costs or price reductions.[3] Hence, return, risk and liquidity are the so-called "magic triangle" of asset allocation (see Figure 2-1).

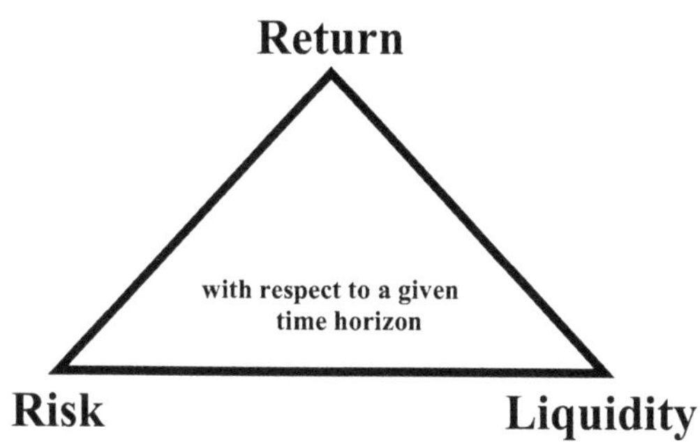

Figure 2-1: The magic triangle of asset allocation

[2] SPREMANN (2008), p. 15.
[3] SPREMANN (2008), p. 2.

The return is obviously one of the most common parameters in finance. It reveals the investment results and is often expressed as a percentage of the invested amount. The return can be defined as being arithmetic or continuous. Asset allocation is generally based on arithmetic returns. Moreover, the differentiation between an achieved and an expected return is crucial. As one might expect, the achieved return refers to the past, whereas the expected return is a target dimension of an investment. Consequently, asset allocation requires return expectations for an investment period in the future.

Risk is a kind of insecurity,[4] but offers negative as well as positive deviation of something expected. In the asset allocation context and portfolio theory, risk is often defined as the variation of random arithmetic returns from the estimated return and measured as the standard deviation.[5] Thus, risk per se is an undesired and disadvantageous effect, especially in relation with an economic activity. Referring to a broader context, several kinds of risk such as market risk, political risk, interest rate risk and currency risk affect the asset allocation process.[6] However, in finance risk is normally measured as a standard deviation and includes positive as well as negative deviations.[7] Therefore, insecurity in asset allocation also offers potential.

Diversification is an important effect reducing the risk in portfolio optimization. The correlation coefficients of asset classes are a hint for diversification. These coefficients measure the relation of asset returns. Two highly correlated asset classes such as equities world and equities emerging markets rarely allow massive risk reduction. The returns of both asset classes have a positive correlation. However, cat bonds are almost uncorrelated to financial market risks except liquidity. Hence they have an attractive diversification potential. Asset class diversification effects have a vast impact on asset allocation in modern portfolio theory.[8] The realization of optimal portfolio diversification is merely possible, if all potential asset

---

[4] Insecurity is a broader term, whereas the term risk implies information about the underlying distribution of the insecure parameter.

[5] SPREMANN & GANTENBEIN (2005), p. 75.

[6] For example, a detailed overview and assessment of market, credit and operational risks is outlined in the Basel II documentations (BIS 2004 and 2005).

[7] Consequently some researchers have proposed to implement a new risk measure in finance, the semi-variance (see MARKOWITZ (1959), pp. 188 or COPELAND & WESTON (1988), pp. 152).

[8] However, in a crisis the correlation of asset classes sometimes increases dramatically. In October 2008, liquidity constrains of investors caused a dramatic increase of correlation.

classes are taken into consideration.[9] Therefore, an increased range of asset classes reduces the anticipated risk of the portfolio and hence allows investors to hold superior portfolios with less risk or higher returns.

Liquidity is a further key measure in asset allocation. In basic model portfolios and capital market theory, liquidity is not considered as a parameter.[10] Nevertheless investors do have a strict preference for investments that can be liquidated easily without high transaction costs. Therefore, the bid-ask spread is widely used as a proxy for liquidity. However, for various asset classes the bid-ask spread increases in crises situations.[11] In fact the rebalancing of a portfolio especially in crises situations is only possible with liquid investments. Accordingly liquidity aspects are essential in a practical environment due to rebalancing and redemption aspects.

The portfolio allocation is primarily defined by these three parameters. In addition, more investor specific input parameters have to be considered. This may include an initial time horizon, the utility preference or risk aversion, the investment plan as well as the level of the investors' activity and knowledge. As a consequence, return, risk and liquidity assumptions have to be specified for every considered asset class. Moreover, a sound knowledge of the owners' interests is required. Therefore asset allocation deals with a sound weighting of return, risk and liquidity to meet investors' needs.[12] As a result, asset allocation specialists apply quantitative methods of portfolio theory to optimize portfolios of institutional and private clients.

Top-down versus bottom-up

Investors can take a top-down or a bottom-up perspective on asset allocation. While consequent asset allocation goes hand in hand with a top-down strategy, sometimes private investors follow a bottom-up approach.[13] Institutional and sophisticated

---

[9] AUCKENTHALER (1991), p. 286.

[10] Some researchers tried to close that gap. SHARPE and ALEXANDER for example developed a CAPM including liquidity aspects (SHARPE/ALEXANDER/BAILEY (1999), pp. 248).

[11] In the financial crises equities with large capitalizations and government bonds from AAA-rated countries remained the only very liquid investment. For example, even inflation linked bonds of the USA or France had a bid-ask spread of about 1.5% - if tradable at all. Many brokers were not able to take any risk at all and hence did not participate in the markets.

[12] SPREMANN (2008), p. 5.

[13] SPREMANN (2008), pp. 15.

private investors determine their portfolio allocation on asset class level. Subsequently, investment decisions on country, sector and security selection level are made. However, private investors sometimes tend to invest bottom-up with a stock- or asset-picking approach without a structured investment process. Obviously a consequent asset allocation comes along with a top-down approach.

Strategic and tactical asset allocation

A further differentiation of asset allocation is the time horizon. In practice, asset allocation is often divided in a strategic and tactical perspective. A strategic asset allocation (SAA) is a long-term positioning of a portfolio, which is derived by optimizing investors' needs.[14] However, despite a long-term optimization, sometimes markets encourage to take short term deviations of a long-term perspective. These temporary shifts are called tactical asset allocation (TAA).[15] Furthermore, a TAA can be more detailed regarding asset classes, countries and sectors.[16]

Dynamic or insured asset allocation strategies are specifications of a TAA approach. Routine processes are applied as part of a continuing asset allocation. Despite the strategic buy- and hold-approach, rebalancing, structured tactical decision making and portfolio insurance strategies such as constant proportion portfolio insurance (CPPI) are approaches integrating also a tactical asset allocation concept.

Academic research and practical experience indicate a dominance of the SAA in terms of performance and meeting investors' needs.[17] Additionally, tactical decisions and concepts may fine-tune strategic portfolio positioning as well as single security selection.

2.2 Portfolio theory

Portfolio theory provides quantitative tools for asset allocation decisions. As discussed, the return maximization is rarely the ultimate goal. Moreover, an optimised

---

[14] SPREMANN (2008), p. 15.

[15] LGT Capital Management implements such a strategic and tactical asset allocation framework for various balanced mandates and portfolios. However, depending on time horizon and style, in some portfolios SAA dominates TAA or vice versa.

[16] STEINER & BRUNS (2007), p. 109.

[17] BRINSON ET. AL. (1985).

risk-adjusted return that meets investors' utility preferences (including liquidity) is the aim.

In portfolio theory, several quantitative optimization processes exist to obtain an optimal portfolio. The selection of an adequate concept is crucial to develop a sound asset allocation. However, the concepts differ in the underlying assumptions regarding the asset class parameters, market factors and investor parameters to perform the optimization.[18] The vast majority of optimization concepts require at least return, risk and correlation parameters for all asset classes. Additionally, some information regarding the investors' utility preference is essential, which can be proxied by an investors' risk parameter.

2.2.1 Mean-variance concept

More than 50 years ago, Harry Markowitz (1952) revolutionized the portfolio theory. In his articles and books he outlines the optimal portfolio within the mean-variance framework.[19] Given return expectations as well as variance and covariance of returns, Markowitz extrapolates an efficient frontier in a risk-return matrix. The optimal portfolio can be found by maximizing the expected return minus some multiple of variance. This μ/σ-optimization of returns of risky assets is the standard approach and basis of the modern portfolio theory (MPT).[20]

The portfolio return in a mean-variance optimization with two assets – here equities and bonds – is described by the returns of the two assets. The risk parameter consists of the assets' standard deviations and the correlation of the assets:

$$R_p(x) = x * R_E + (1-x) * R_B$$

$$\mu_p(x) = x * \mu_E + (1-x) * \mu_B$$

$$\sigma_p^2(x) = x^2 * \sigma_E^2 + (1-x)^2 * \sigma_E^2 + 2 * x * (1-x) * \sigma_E * \sigma_B * \rho_{E,B}$$

when x is the weight of equities, *(1-x)* is the weight of bonds, R is defined as the return, μ is the expected return, σ being the standard deviation of an asset and $\rho_{E,B}$ is defined as the correlation of the returns of equities and bonds.

---

[18] Typical examples are distribution of returns, market efficiency and investors' rationality.
[19] MARKOWITZ (1952, 1959 and 1987).
[20] A detailed introduction is outlined in SPREMANN & GANTENBEIN (2005), pp. 82.

The asset allocation of an investor should maximize the portfolio return with respect to his utility function, here described with the risk aversion parameter λ:

$$\Phi[R_P(x)] = E[R_P(x)] - \frac{\lambda}{2} * \text{var}[R_P(x)]$$

whereas $\Psi(x) = \Phi[R_P(x)]$ is a concave function of the first asset, in the following example of the equity quota. If no restrictions apply, the maximum is determined by setting the first derivative $\Psi'(x)$ equal to zero:

$$\Psi'(x) = (\mu_{E-}\mu_B) - \lambda[x * (\sigma_E^2 + \sigma_B^2 - 2 * \sigma_E * \sigma_B * \rho_{E,B})] - \sigma_B^2 + \sigma_E * \sigma_B * \rho_{E,B}$$

with $\Psi'(x) = 0$ an optimal equity quota applies

$$x = \frac{\frac{\mu_E - \mu_B}{\lambda} + (\sigma_B^2 - \sigma_E * \sigma_B * \rho_{E,B})}{\sigma_E^2 + \sigma_B^2 - 2 * \sigma_E * \sigma_B * \rho_{E,B}}$$

In a more general form, the optimization identifies the optimal portfolio with a maximum return for investors with a certain risk tolerance measured by the standard deviation of arithmetic returns. Accordingly, the portfolio maximization problem is as follows:[21]

$$\mu_p(x_1, x_2, ..., x_n) = \sum_{k=1}^{n} x_k * \mu_k \rightarrow \max!$$

subject to

$s = \sigma_p(x_1, x_2, ..., x_n)$ and

$x_1 + x_2 + ... + x_n = 1$.

The result of the maximization process is the efficient frontier. The efficient frontier illustrates all optimal portfolios (see Figure 2-2). Thus, according to Markowitz' theory the rational investor selects the portfolio from the efficient frontier under the restrictions of his utility or risk preferences.

[21] SPREMANN (2008), p. 188.

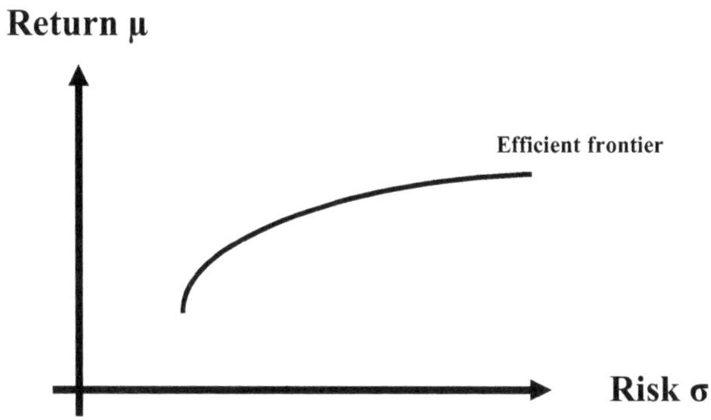

Figure 2-2: Efficient frontier

The mean-variance approach can be implemented for strategic asset allocation purposes with several asset classes as well as an optimization process for assets within the same asset category. Yet even though the mean-variance concept has dominated the portfolio selection process, at least academically, the original problem of portfolio theory is how to maximize the expected value of the investors' utility. Moreover, it is a shortcut that solves the problem perfectly under a restrictive set of assumptions such as standard normal distribution of returns or market efficiency.[22]

Markowitz' mean-variance concept is controversially discussed in finance. The main criticism includes that the return distribution is only described by their first two moments.[23] Furthermore, the mean-variance concept is a static, one-period approach and implies a buy-and-hold strategy.[24] Additionally, questions of timing are not covered and investors' restrictions such as home bias, the integration of

[22] UYSAL ET. AL (2001).

[23] One of the first and most prominent critics regarding the assumption of a Gaussian distribution was made by MANDELBROT (1963) and to some extent also by FAMA (1965). Among others CAMPBELL ET. AL (1997, pp. 19) argue to the contrary that long-term returns tend to be closer to the normal distribution, because all moments are finite and the Central Limit Theorem applies. However, alternative asset classes are an integral part of portfolios today and research regarding these asset classes shows clear evidence for non-normal distributed returns (e.g. BROOKS & KAT (2002)). Moreover, SPREMANN (2008) states that long-term returns tend to be log-normally distributed.

[24] Market efficiency, investors' rationality and assumption of static return, risk and correlation parameters for the given period have also been widely criticised. However, REILLY & BROWN (2006, p. 232) argue that a theory should not be judged on the basis of its assumptions but rather on its predictive efficiency.

human capital[25] exposure and social capital[26] are not addressed.[27] With today's computing power, it seems evitable to relax the restrictions[28] and to approach the problem as well with other concepts.

The portfolio theory outlined by Markowitz was extended subsequently. In 1965, Tobin introduced a multi-period mean variance concept. Some years later, Merton published a continuing time approach.[29] William Sharpe, Jack Treynor, John Lintner and Jan Mossin addressed some more of the issues mentioned above and evolved the Capital Asset Pricing Model (CAPM).[30] Later on several extended concepts of the CAPM have been developed. However, Markowitz' theory is the beginning of modern portfolio theory.

2.2.2 Shortfall concept

The shortfall concept is a further portfolio optimization method. According to this theory the breach of a primarily defined investment objective is called shortfall. Investors have varying investment objectives. As a result, there are several definitions of shortfalls. The three main categories of shortfalls focus on return, wealth or the coverage ratio in pension finance.[31] Firstly, a shortfall can be defined as a breach of a defined minimum return in a defined period. Secondly, a specific minimum wealth can be defined as a constraint of the portfolio optimization. If in a specified period the investors' wealth shrinks below the defined objective, a shortfall occurs. Thirdly, pension funds have to fulfil an asset allocation with respect to in- and outflows as well as performance. Therefore, the coverage ratio[32] can be defined as a trigger for a shortfall. As a result, the shortfall concept is a broad approach that can be adapted to investor specific needs.[33]

---

[25] SPREMANN (1997, 1995) as well as HORNEFF ET. AL. (2009).

[26] COLEMAN (1990) describes social capital as a prerequisite for human capital. LANG (2009) follows this argumentation and connects it to private equity and venture capital performance.

[27] LANG (2009), p. 5.

[28] In addition to the criticisms mentioned above, transaction costs or even taxes as well as a credit limit can be implemented in the optimization process.

[29] TOBIN (1965) and MERTON (1969, 1990).

[30] SHARPE (1964), TREYNOR (1962), LINTNER (1965) and MOSSIN (1966).

[31] ZIMMERMANN (2004), p. 19.

[32] This indicator measures to what extent pension funds can meet their future financial obligations.

[33] GANTENBEIN ET. AL (2001, pp. 95) provide an applied insight.

The definition of a minimum return is for a wide range of investors a key parameter. In the mean-variance context, Markowitz defined the variance as a risk parameter. However, preferences of investors are not correctly described, because upside volatility is not perceived as a negative risk. The upside volatility provides investors with a small benefit, whereas the downside volatility exhibits a major disadvantage.[34] To capture this non-linear utility function, the shortfall concept offers the possibility to optimize a portfolio focusing on downside risk.

Roy shortfall concept

In 1952 Roy published an article about investors' risk perception and optimal portfolios.[35] Roy defines a minimum return t_{roy} as a key parameter for an investors' risk. Obviously the probability of breaching this minimum return in a defined time horizon shall be minimized. If portfolios are characterized by return and variance expectations, the shortfall probability can be calculated by using the Chebyshev's inequality[36]:

$$p(t_{Roy}) \equiv prob(R \leq t_{Roy}) \leq prob(|R - \mu(R)| \geq \mu(R) - t_{Roy}) \leq \frac{\sigma^2(R)}{\left[\mu(R) - t_{Roy}\right]^2}$$

The equivalent to the minimization of the upper bound $-\frac{\sigma^2(R)}{\left[\mu(R) - t_{Roy}\right]^2}$ is the maximization of the term $\frac{\mu(R) - t_{Roy}}{\sigma(R)}$. As a result, a straight line with the slope s can be defined

$$\mu(R) = -s * \sigma(R) + t_{Roy}$$

and introduced into a mean-variance framework. In this context, the minimum return is the intersection of the function with the ordinate. The steepness of the slope s indicates the shortfall probability, whereby steepness and shortfall probability are negatively correlated. Ideally, the shortfall line is a tangent line to the efficient

[34] See footnote 7.

[35] Interestingly, it was published more or less simultaneously with MARKOWITZ' concept. Until today, MARKOWITZ is suspected of plagiarism.

[36] The Russian mathematician PAFNUTY CHEBYSHEV (1821-1894) is widely known for his contribution in the field of probability, statistics and number theory.

frontier.[37] The resulting portfolio is often referred to as Roy or safety-first portfolio (see Figure 2-3).

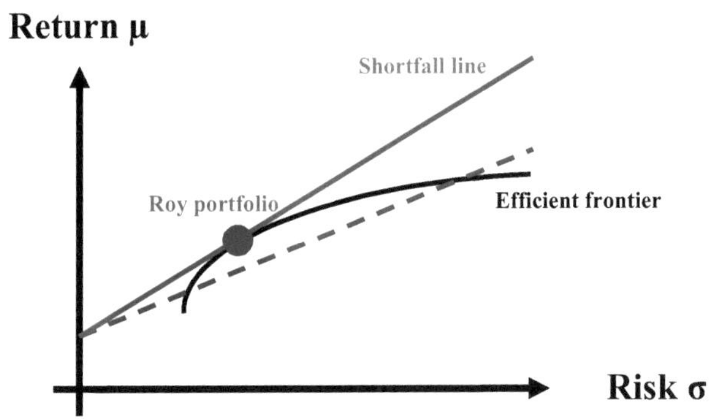

Figure 2-3: Roy shortfall concept

Kataoka shortfall concept

A different shortfall concept was introduced by Kataoka (1963). He suggests allowing a breach of the minimum return objective by a previously defined probability. As a result, in a first step a probability for a breach has to be defined. In a second step, the minimum return parameter can be maximized. In contrast to Roy, the steepness of the shortfall line, the shortfall probability, is fixed. The optimal portfolio can be found by a parallel shift of the shortfall line – a maximization of the minimum return target. Again, the shortfall line is a tangent line to the efficient frontier (see Figure 2-4).

---

[37] A more detailed mathematical insight is given by KADUFF (1996).

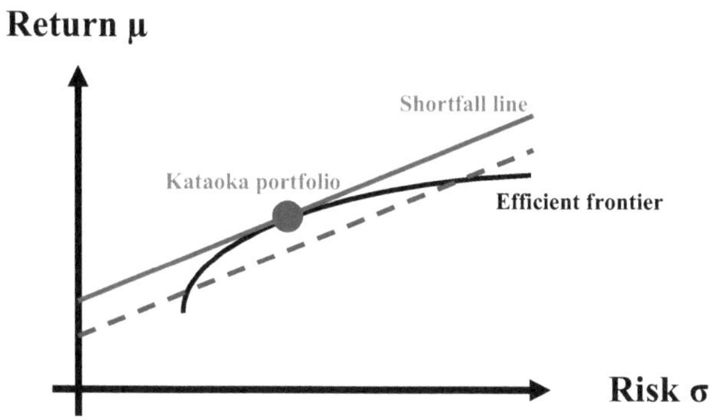

Figure 2-4: Kataoka shortfall concept

Telser shortfall concept

Telser (1955) introduced a shortfall concept that combines the approaches of Roy and Kataoka. According to Telser, an investor should define a minimum return as well as a maximum shortfall. In an optimization process, the portfolio with the highest return fulfilling both restrictions is chosen. However, it might happen that the constraints are too restrictive and the shortfall line cannot be a tangent line of the efficient frontier (see Figure 2-5). In this case, the objectives of the investor cannot be met.

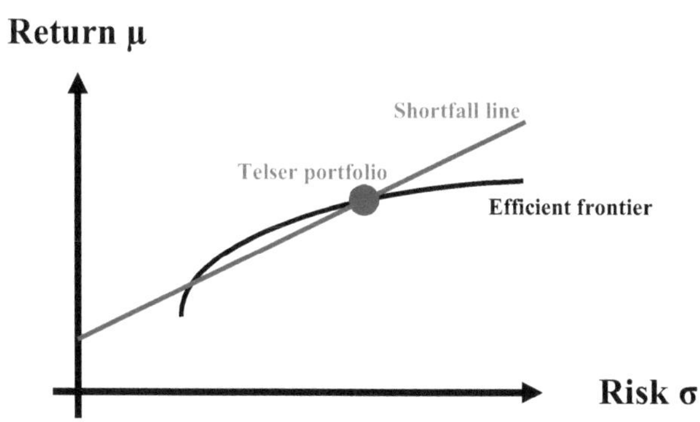

Figure 2-5: Telser shortfall concept

The shortfall concept has two main advantages. On the one hand, it intuitively meets investors' needs and offers plausible constraints. On the other hand, it allows optimizations under the assumption of normally distributed returns as well as randomly distributed returns, if some extensions are integrated.[38] Therefore, the shortfall concept is an adequate complement to Markowitz' mean-variance approach. In conclusion, the definitions of Roy, Kataoka and Telser offer investor specific shortfall and asset allocation solutions.

2.3 Investors' utility preference and categorization

The utility preferences of investors differ widely. The investment objectives range from capital preservation to long-term wealth generation. This heterogeneity needs to be expressed and included into an asset allocation process. In MPT, traditional optimization considers only mean and variance. If those two characteristics are to consider the investors' preferences, returns have to be normally distributed and the utility function of the form:

$$u(r) = \frac{e^{-2\lambda r} - 1}{-2\lambda}$$

With $u(r)$ being the utility of a return r and λ (lambda) a constant of an investors' degree of risk aversion.[39] Consequently, a certain lambda considers different investor types. On the one hand, a λ of 1 maximizes the long-term return of a portfolio but reflects only very little regard for risk. On the other hand the lambda increases with the amount of risk taken into account. Commonly, lambdas of 1-10 apply for asset allocation purposes.[40]

Furthermore, a differentiation of institutional and private investors seems adequate. Private clients are private individuals, whereas institutional clients are pension funds, insurances, banks and companies with financial assets. As one might expect, several factors such as investment goals, know-how and liquidity prefer-

---

[38] The Chebychev inequality allows optimizing without any assumptions of the return distribution. Furthermore, specific return distributions can be assumed (see for example KADUFF (1996) or KALIN & ZAGST (1999)).

[39] UYSAL ET. AL (2001).

[40] See for example UYSAL ET. AL (2001).

ences differ. Therefore, an investor categorization underlines the specific needs of an asset allocation process.

2.3.1 Private investors

One possible segmentation parameter of private clients is the wealth. In literature, a pyramid structure with not exactly selective segments applies.[41] At the bottom of the pyramid are retail clients with less than roughly 1 million of financial assets.[42] These can be further subdivided in three different segments of retail clients. Individuals with more than about 1 million financial assets are private clients especially served by banks. This category can also be subdivided in three groups according to their wealth – affluent clients (1-5 million), high net worth investors (5-20 million) and ultra high net worth individuals (20-50 million). Finally, private investors with more than 50 million financial assets are often represented by a family office (see Figure 2-6).

[41] See for example SPREMANN (2008), p. 29.

[42] The amounts are given in USD. However, since the segmentation is not exact, one could also think in EUR or CHF terms.

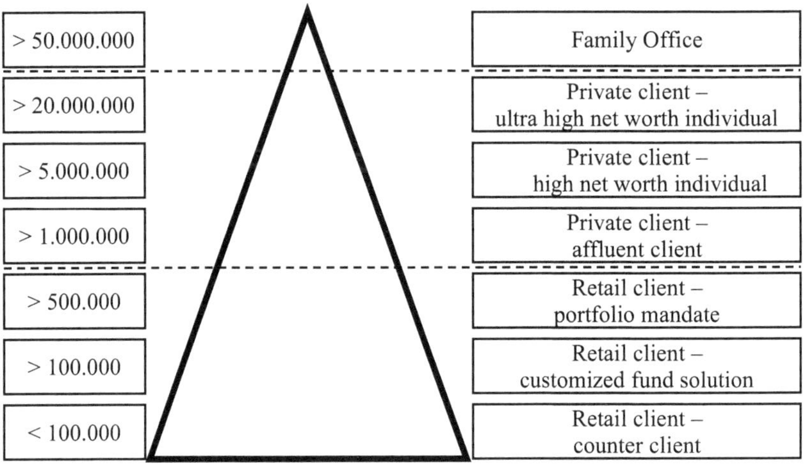

Figure 2-6: Client segmentation of private investors

Risk aversion and/or time horizon of an investment are further segmentation factors for private investors. In fact, these parameters are an integral part of portfolio theory optimization processes. As a consequence, both factors are particularly suitable as private investor segmentation criteria in an asset allocation context. Additionally, a high consistency of both segmentation methods can be expected. In the following paragraphs, three main categories of private investors are introduced.

Very risk-averse private investor

The very risk-averse private investor seeks stability with capital preservation and is less concerned about growth of final wealth. These investors are focused on just a few asset classes and regarding to their relatively low wealth also limited in the investment selection. In the vast majority, these investors are retail clients with no detailed finance know-how.

In portfolio theory these characteristics transfer into a risk aversion parameter lambda of about 10.[43] Furthermore, in a Telser shortfall environment they correspond to a portfolio with no expected loss over a period of about three years and a shortfall risk of 5%.

Risk-averse wealthy private investor

The risk-averse wealthy private investor aims for stability with some potential for increased investment value. These investors came into wealth or have accumulated it in their professional life. Financial advisors or banks propose investment schemes and include various asset classes. In most cases, the result is a diversified portfolio with a broad investment space.

The risk aversion factor in a portfolio theory context is roughly a lambda of 3.25. In that case, in a Telser shortfall environment a portfolio with no expected loss over a period of five years and a shortfall risk of 5% applies.

Long-term investing family office

Family offices, a third category of individual investments, prefer a long-term growth potential. Even though family offices are an entity, its main business is to implement the investment objectives of a private person. The company is managed by several investment professionals and allows a complex investment structure including all asset classes and investment possibilities. As a consequence, the portfolio of a family office is very well-diversified.

Family offices demand for long-term returns and hence the risk aversion factor in a portfolio theory context is low with a lambda of about 1. Accordingly, in a Telser shortfall environment, a portfolio with no expected loss over a period of about ten years and a shortfall risk of 5% is implemented.

2.3.2 Institutional investors

Institutional investors are professionals for instance pension funds, insurance companies or financial institutions. Investment specialist with various backgrounds and investment expertises work for these entities. Generally, formal investment

---

[43] The risk aversion parameter lambda and the Telser criteria set for this and the following investor types are backwards engineered and derived according investor type congruent portfolio weights of chapter 6.

processes exist and a supervisory authority controls investments as well as processes. Furthermore, an institutional investor allocates a considerable amount of money often more than one billion USD. As a result, normally all investable asset classes are considered and hence the asset allocation of institutional investors is sophisticated. However, for some institutional investors regulatory restrictions do apply.

Pension fund

Pension funds seek long-term steady growth potential. However, a sound asset-liability as well as cash management is required. The investment board has professional investment advisors and delegates the portfolio management to specialists. Consequently, one would expect a very well-diversified portfolio. But in a lot of countries certain investment restrictions apply.[44] These often include a home bias and in some countries a quote for sustainable investments.[45] As a result, the portfolio underlies several restrictions and in practice the asset allocation cannot be perfectly optimized.

Pension funds are interested in stable returns, but have clear investment restrictions. The risk aversion factor in a portfolio theory context is roughly a lambda of 2. Correspondingly, in a Telser shortfall environment, a portfolio with no expected loss over a period of about seven years applies.

State investment fund

State investment funds are very long-term investors seeking a high growth potential. Such a fund manages at least several billions and some of them even close to a trillion USD.[46] Thus, the investment strategy is well-diversified and includes also very illiquid as well as some high risk investments. In general, state investment

[44] The „Verordnung über die berufliche Alters-, Hinterlassenen- und Invalidenvorsorge" (BVV2) sets the investment guidelines for Swiss pension funds. The BVV2 lists allowed asset classes (Art. 53) and as well sets restrictions for each and combinations of those (Art. 54).

[45] This is the case in Scandinavian countries and becomes increasingly popular.

[46] The Abu Dhabi Investment Authority (ADIA) is estimated to allocate more than USD 800 billion. A recent overview of state investment funds was given by MASLAKOVIC (2009) from International Financial Services London (IFSL).

funds embark on a strategy based on financial objectives. Nevertheless some also follow strategic goals.[47]

The long-term investment horizon allows state investment funds a low risk aversion factor lambda of about 0.5. Accordingly, in a Telser shortfall environment, a portfolio with no expected loss over a period of up to 15 years is appropriate.

2.4 Asset allocation requirements

Portfolio optimization requires specific input parameters. This includes return, standard deviation and correlation estimations for every considerable asset class. These assumptions are often based on past data. Furthermore, parameters regarding the investors' utility preferences, the time horizon and the liquidity of the specific asset classes have to be considered. As a result, several problems arise.

The most obvious problem is: Past performance is no indication for future performance. However, in practice generally an analysis of a longer time period in the past is taken as a proxy for the future. The time period should include at least one economic cycle for every specific asset class as well as a major crisis situation. This allows analyzing the returns in different economic regimes. As a result, an analysis of at least 20 years is recommended to get meaningful data for the derivation of estimations.

In practice, the past is generally taken for expectations. In a sophisticated asset allocation framework, several regimes are defined and the return of similar past regimes attributed. This allocation of returns to regimes is problematic. No macroeconomic situation is unique and it is undoubted that the every boom or crisis is specific. For example, inflationary regimes are often proxied by periods in 1970s an 1980s. However, since these decades several global factors have changed dramatically such as geopolitical powershifts, cross-linkage of capital markets, goods markets and even human capital. Accordingly the estimated parameters in the different regimes are disputable. But at least such an asset allocation framework allows

[47] The Chinese Investment Corporation clearly has financial and strategic goals, whereas the Norwegian Government Pension Fund – Global ("the petroleum fund") follows a strictly performance driven strategy.

expectations about the weighting of regimes[48]. In conclusion, the input parameters for asset allocation optimizations are questionable.

New or young asset classes face even more problems in asset allocation. The past experience of only a few months or years cannot provide a sound indication, as the asset class has not shown its characteristics in several states of an economic cycle. This affects more asset classes than one might think. For example data series for emerging market bonds are available from around 1990 or cat bonds from 2001. Additionally, young markets and asset classes have a strong tendency to undergo major changes such as regulatory issues, market size impacts or synergy effects. For this reason, a quantitative estimation of input parameters for portfolio optimization is not an appropriate approach.

On top of this, several problems with past data apply. On the one hand this is availability. As aforementioned, for various asset classes data series are only available for the last decades. Even government bond data for Germany or the United Kingdom prior to 1960 are very hard to get. On the other hand, these data are often subject to various problems. For example hedge funds indices are affected by survivorship biases, self-selection bias and backfill bias.[49] As a result, the use of historic data as an indication of future performance also includes the challenge to make use of the appropriate ones.

In the following chapters, a qualitative methodology to generate the asset class specific input parameters is outlined and hence, new asset classes can also be integrated in quantitative portfolio theory models.

2.5 Summary

An appropriate asset allocation is an essential element for any investor. Thereby a huge variety of different asset classes from equity and government bond investments to private equity and hedge funds or even less known catastrophe bonds can

[48] See also chapter 3.5.

[49] Many hedge funds have a short life and hence they are excluded from indices generating a survivorship bias. Furthermore, for some indices the participation of funds is voluntary and a self-selection bias occurs. Moreover, new funds reporting to an index might be allowed to report also prior data. This of course only happens, if the performance was good and hence a backfill bias results. A detailed overview is outlined in LHABITANT (2004), pp. 87.

be considered. The match of investors' return expectations, risk and liquidity preferences and investment horizon with a sound combination of those asset classes is the main goal of asset allocation. For that reason, different investor categories require distinct solutions. However, a major limitation in asset allocation is the complexity. The information available to meet investors' needs is backward-looking. The challenge is to develop a comprehensive forward-looking approach dealing with the complexity of the unknown.

3 Scenario Approach in Asset Allocation

3.1 Idea of scenario analysis

Strategic decisions in private, public and non-profit sectors are based on expectations regarding future developments. Therefore, the creation of strategic concepts depends on certain assumptions. Scenario planning is a powerful tool that can improve the quality of such strategic long-term decision making.[50]

Scenario methods have been used in military and strategic management for decades. [51] Following World War II, the US Air Force introduced scenario methodologies as a tool for military planning. In the 1960s, the military strategist Herman Kahn transferred and adapted scenario techniques for business strategy and planning. Yet scenario methodologies only entered a new dimension in the early 1970s. Pierre Wack worked in the Group Planning department of Royal Dutch/Shell in London.[52] Among others, his unit analysed a scenario of rapidly rising oil prices against market expectation of stable prices. In a snapshot, Wack and his team believed that the Islamic countries could dictate the oil price and would do so, if Western countries offended them. In a scenario, the whole impact on the oil business and Royal Dutch/Shell specifically was outlined. Even though executives did not give that scenario a high likelihood, they were emotionally prepared for dramatic changes. A few months later after the "Yom Kippur" war in October 1973, prices rose dramatically and Royal Dutch/Shell was the only oil company with strategies at hand as well as executives who were prepared for such a scenario. The scenario strategist Pierre Wack and the executives partnered in making Royal Dutch/Shell become one of the largest and most profitable oil companies.[53]

Scenario thinking is an interdisciplinary method to develop a set of various possible futures in a complex environment. Michael Porter defines scenarios as "an internally consistent view of what the future might turn out to be – not a forecast,

[50] MINX & ROEHL (2006), p. 78.
[51] MINX & ROEHL (2006), p. 78.
[52] WACK later published two papers on this Royal Dutch/Shell scenario case in HARVARD BUSINESS REVIEW.
[53] SCHWARTZ (1996), pp. 7.

but one possible future outcome".[54] The extraordinary social, governmental and economic changes in modern times require planning tools that can deal with complexity and hence improve the quality of decision making.[55] However, coherent scenarios are a first step in a strategy development process. The critical phase is the following extrapolation of strategic options as a result of various scenarios.[56]

The practical link of scenarios to strategic planning is a key element. Scenarios are a tool for strategy and analysis. Ringland suggests several different uses for scenarios in a strategic context.[57] Firstly, scenario thinking is a powerful tool for strategy development. Secondly, scenarios are a helpful tool in strategy evaluations for testing existing strategies. Additionally, scenarios can also be used to develop hedging or contingency plans. Finally, the accomplishment of a risk assessment of a project or across a portfolio of businesses is possible. In general, scenarios can be used in a broad context in strategy and strategic planning.

In addition, scenario techniques allow extensive insights. The comprehensive approach explores uncertainties and allows prioritizing issues of potential concerns. Moreover, emerging risks and opportunities are discovered even if signals are weak. Scenarios also overcome the hierarchy and bureaucracy of an organization. The team approach creates a common language and results in a shared view and will to implement. Furthermore, scenario thinking focuses the attention in the process more on external challenges than internal issues. Hence, surprises are revealed and one is prepared to act accordingly. Apart from this, scenario processes provide a forum for learning and exchanging thoughts – for individuals, teams and corporations. In fact, this often has a significant impact in the long-term.[58]

A scenario funnel illustrates the methodology of a scenario technique (see Figure 3-1). Starting from present, paths defined by several underlying factors create various possible futures. In a long time horizon, the extreme scenarios diverge more from the present state than in the short term. Additionally, the number of underlying factors and periods increases the quantity of potential futures. As a result, a selec-

---

[54] PORTER (1985, p. 63).
[55] MINX & BÖHLKE (2006), p. 14.
[56] WEF (2009a), p. 77.
[57] RINGLAND (1998), p. 111.
[58] RINGLAND (2002), pp. 75.

tion process keeps the number of analyzed potential futures neat.[59] However, the selection follows some rules to provide a diversified mix of scenarios. Finally, at least two and up to five scenarios are developed for a specific question.

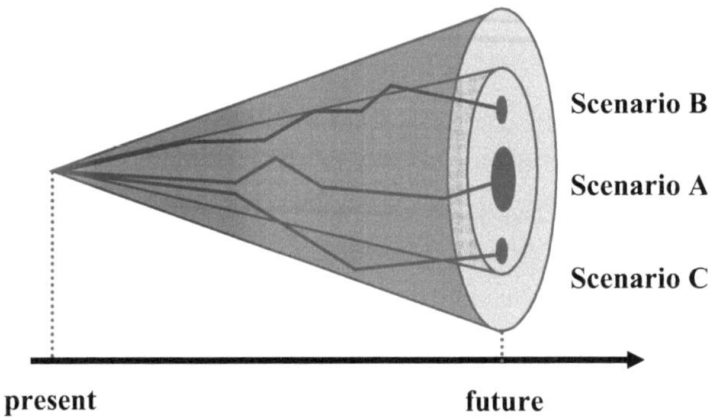

Figure 3-1: Scenario funnel

Scenario methodologies are applied for corporate strategic purposes mainly in four different fields. Firstly, these techniques are used to detect and describe political and economic changes. Another focus area is industry restructuring. Scenario thinking is also adapted to issues regarding new products or markets. Finally in the corporate sector scenario work has been used to refine business portfolios. Furthermore, environmental studies have been conducted with a scenario approach by NGOs and the public sector as well as public policy studies.[60] In fact, scenario techniques have been applied to various fields and issues in the corporate, public and non-profit sectors.

---

[59] MISSLER-BEHR (in WILMS (2006)) provides a detailed approach for a quantitatively based selection of scenarios in the scenario funnel. However, this approach does not fit for qualitatively driven processes. In these cases other methodologies apply, one will be described in the following chapter.

[60] RINGLAND (2002), pp. 79.

3.2 The scenario process

A scenario process is clearly structured in several steps. In literature and practice, different process descriptions exist. However, the objective, approach and structure of the described methodologies are quite similar. In some steps several executable tools exist. A main differentiation criterion is often a more qualitative or more quantitative driven approach. In general, most scenario processes are structured in eight steps. In the following, a standardized process according to Minx/Roehl is outlined (see Figure 3-2).[61]

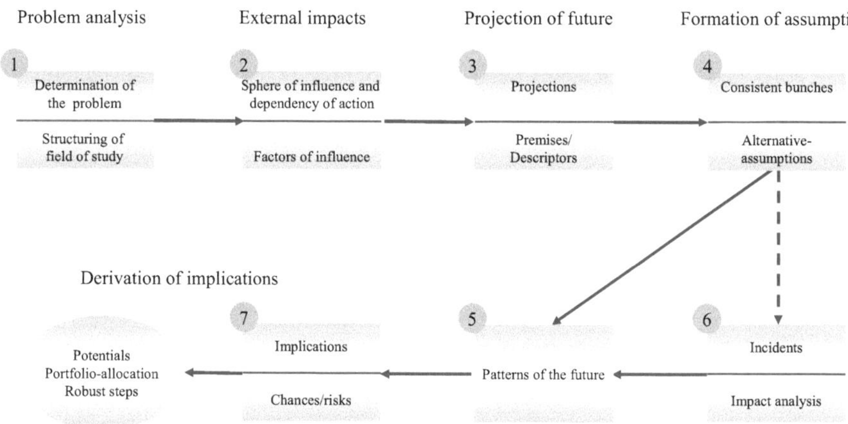

Figure 3-2: Steps of a standard scenario approach[62]

The first step is a clear determination of the topic including a specification of the research area. The starting point of every scenario process is the definition of the problem set. Next, the field of study has to be specified factual, temporal and areal. The process of defining and specifying a problem set for a scenario question is a key element. All following steps refer to this question. As a result, the definition of

[61] MINX & ROEHL (2006) provide an overview of a methodology often used by scenario experts of Daimler AG. Other valuable insights into the steps of scenario processes are provided by GOTTSCHALK & STEINBRECHER (2005) and SCHWARTZ (1996, pp. 241).

[62] According to MINX & ROEHL (2006).

the right question from the beginning is a very important element in a scenario process.

In a second step, external impact factors influencing the problem set are gathered. This listing of key factors and driving forces includes various topics such as economic, social and political indicators, environmental or technical factors, industry-related issues and specific factors of a business area or company. This determination of key forces is completed by a qualitative as well as a quantitative definition of these factors. Usually a coherent set of 20 up to more than 100 key forces can be brainstormed and defined by the participants of a scenario process.

Thereafter trend projections are estimated for all factors gathered. On the one hand this enables the group to get a deep and equal understanding of the factors. On the other hand the participants develop two to three states of all these factors according to the time frame of the problem set. At the end of step three the key drivers and forces are gathered, defined and potential future states are described.

In a fourth step, these factors get ranked by uncertainty and impact. All participants give points on a scale from 0-2 for uncertainty and for impact to every factor. The aggregated sum of all participants is the score for each factor. As a result, all factors and driving forces can be placed in an uncertainty-impact matrix (see Figure 3-3). The idea is to identify two or three factors that are most uncertain and have a high impact. Uncertain factors define flexible states in the future, whereas predetermined factors such as the demography (in the short and medium term) have an equal state in all scenarios. Consequently, factors with high uncertainty create in a matrix four possible scenario fields. In addition, high impact factors ensure that key forces for the problem set are chosen. As a result, the uncertainty-impact matrix identifies factors that span a scenario cross with different scenario fields (see Figure 3-3). However, the determination of these axes is complicated, but it represents an essential part in the scenario process. In conclusion the uncertainty-impact analysis supports the selection of two descriptors for the scenario matrix axes. Hence, this step defines the main framework of the scenarios.

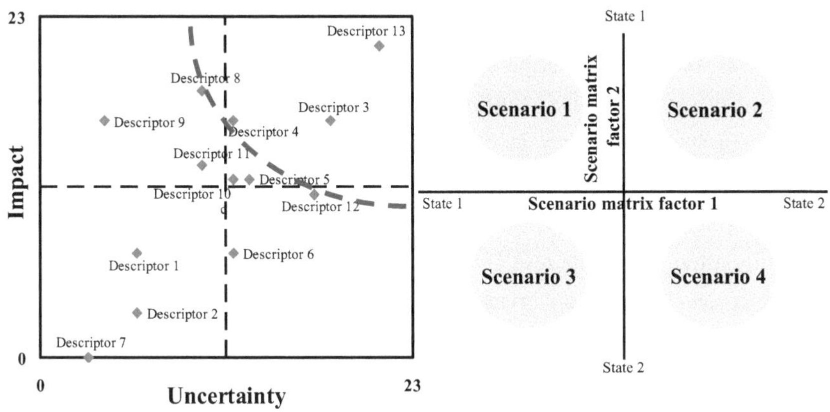

Figure 3-3: Uncertainty-impact matrix and scenario matrix

In the next step, scenarios are developed in detail. Therefore a scenario cross is spanned with two axes and four scenario fields. The axes are defined by two factors selected in the uncertainty-impact analysis (see Figure 3-3). These key parameters are described by two or three potential future outcomes. In general, a 2x2 matrix applies, but in some circumstances it is necessary to generate more scenarios with a 2x3 or even a 3x3 scenario matrix. Subsequently all gathered impact factors and key forces are described in every field of the scenario matrix. This process needs specific attention as it influences the specific character of the scenarios. For example, a definition of the macroeconomic conditions is not predetermined in any scenario. However, a balanced scenario process often generates outcomes for different economic situations. Therefore, while creating a specific scenario, interdependencies with the other scenarios have to be taken into account. As a result, well-defined scenarios are formed and edited with all key parameters identified by the scenario process.

The sixth step integrates extreme scenarios to the process. The participants develop so-called "wild card scenarios" or "black swans", which have radical consequences for the problem set and are often triggered only by one or two parameters. This creates awareness for rapid as well as unexpected changes and is a key component of a scenario process.

Thereafter the consequences and implications of the determined scenarios for the problem set are analysed. Furthermore, opportunities, risks and courses of action in respect of the scenarios are identified. A definition of best practices as well as a check for a specific strategy in each scenario reveals strengths and weaknesses. Moreover, a robustness check for strategies across all scenarios gives an intention of the underlying risks.

Finally, a transfer of the results into business needs takes place. For example, a strategy is developed or an existing strategy adapted according to the generated scenarios. In addition, leading indicators and signposts are defined. Periodically these factors are monitored and support the identification of the scenario the real world develops closest to.

In general, some additional considerations are important for a scenario process. Firstly an elaborated selection of the scenario team of about 10-15 participants is crucial. The decision criteria are the inclusion of executive people that support the results of the process, a broad diversification regarding know-how and background and the participation of imaginative, open minded and team-oriented persons. Secondly, the development of more than just two scenarios as well as at least one wild card scenario enables more plausible results with regards to the scenario funnel. The generation of four scenarios and one wild card scenario is a balanced option to keep a meaningful decision making tool on the one hand, but provide a broad range of scenarios on the other hand. Finally, the relevance and persuasive power of a scenario process is heavily dependent on the groups' ability to create plausible, but also surprising scenarios. Moreover, the scenario team has to take the ownership to integrate the results into the strategic decision making process. In fact, a scenario process is a complex tool, whose achievement is often on a knife's edge due to structural, conceptual or personal issues.

3.3 Critical assessment of the scenario approach

A scenario process contains advantages and limitations. However, the tool can be implemented in areas where the advantages outweigh the disadvantages. Therefore the characteristics of scenario methodologies have to be considered.

The scenario process offers advantages for strategic decisions in various fields. A main advantage is the improvement of structural assumptions and data for planning.

Both, assumptions and data, are needed for any strategy decision that deals with decision making under uncertainty. In fact, the scenario process clearly gathers parameters and their circumstances and allows for different future conditions. Thus, this holistic approach allows enhancing the robustness and quality of strategic decisions by discovering and framing uncertainties.

Another key advantage is the possibility to include key decision makers. On the one hand, it generally improves the awareness of change in the company. On the other hand, the key decision makers are emotionally prepared for a change, have been involved in the scenario developing process and hence are ready to embark on a future-oriented strategy.[63]

Well-defined scenarios can also be introduced for communication and marketing purposes. The process generates a multifarious future. As a result, all scenarios or only components such as key factors for a specific problem set are perfect techniques and tools for communication with clients, competitors, consultants, academics or other internal employees.

The most prominent but not obvious advantage is the learning process for involved persons. This learning has two aspects. Firstly, the process creates new informal structures within the team. In companies, this is an undervalued success factor for the implementation of new strategies or projects. The best strategy or project is worthless if the work force acts contrary to the idea. However, a scenario process creates envoys, who will drive the strategy or project. Furthermore, these people have often built up a lasting relation abbreviating the decision making in the future and generating a certain entrepreneurial spirit. Secondly, the scenario process is a forum for learning and exchanging thoughts – it creates a better understanding of today's and tomorrow's world. This enables to think out of the box also beyond the scenario process.

The scenario process has, however, also some drawbacks and limitations. In the previous paragraphs the advantages of such a group process are outlined. In fact, group processes also have major limitations. Firstly, a scenario process is time-consuming and involves a lot of management and expert capacity. Depending on

[63] See for example WEF (2009a), p. 77.

the structure, the problem set and the integration of external expert input, the core scenario process team needs to meet at least three times with several working days and up to over 100 group days. Secondly, the process is influenced by the group dynamics and individual engagement of the participants. Group processes can easily be driven by a specific sentiment and if not intervened adequately, destruct the whole process or at least drive it in a certain direction. Finally, the process is dependent on the knowledge of the participants – either direct scenario process members or external specialists, who can contribute an additional share. Consequently, the selection of the scenario process members is a crucial element and should include parameters such as know-how, mentality, hierarchies and especially diversity.

The openness of scenario analyses may also raise problems. A clear direction is not crucial in all stages of such a process. Sometimes the participants have to give free rein to their thoughts. This is an essential element as the process provides the structure, whereas innovation and futurology have to be integrated by the participants.

In academia, replicability is an important criterion for the acceptance of a methodology. Undeniably, the replication of a scenario process is complicated and nearly impossible. Since the reality is not a laboratory, not only the subject may change, but also the catalysts in form of scenario process participants have gathered more information and learnt from the past. For example this drift is imminent in the scenarios of Royal Dutch/Shell over the decades.[64] However, in theory, if the participants – the catalysts – would have exactly the same information and the world would not have changed, a replication of a scenario analysis might deliver the same results.

Finally, the integration of the scenarios into a strategic concept is a difficult point of interception.[65] The development of conclusive scenarios is a requirement, but the objective is a strategic implementation of the results. Yet the transfer of the potential futures directly into a strategic decision needs a structured process from the very

[64] An overview of some of Royal Dutch/Shell's scenarios of the past decades can be retrieved from www.shell.com.

[65] MINX & ROEHL (1998), p. 170.

beginning. The problem set has to be defined, while already having the derivation of implications in mind. Hence the guidance of scenario experts increases the chance of a successful implementation of a scenario analysis into a strategic framework. As a result, Figure 3-4 highlights the main advantages and limitation of a scenario analysis.

Main advantages of a scenario analysis	Main limitations of a scenario analysis
▪ Learning process for participants ▪ Integration & commitment of decision makers ▪ Integration of broad know-how base (market & company specific) ▪ Useful for communication and marketing ▪ Creates several potential outcomes (dealing with uncertainty)	▪ Time consuming ▪ Cost intensive (primarily indirect costs) ▪ Dependent on group process (e.g. sentiment)

Figure 3-4: Main advantages and limitations of a scenario analysis

3.4 Examples of scenario analyses

Scenario analyses are a widely known though rarely used tool for strategic decision making. However, some companies, e.g. Shell and Daimler, have already taken advantage of this methodology for decades.[66] Moreover, in recent years scenario thinking is implemented by many global companies, government agencies and community agencies as a popular strategy and long-term thinking tool. In the following chapters, two current examples of scenario processes will be outlined.

[66] Shell and Daimler-Benz both launched their scenario process departments in the 1970s.

3.4.1 Scenario analysis "The future of the global financial system"

The World Economic Forum (WEF) launched a scenario planning initiative in 2003. Up to now, several studies applying scenario concepts were published.[67] In 2008, the WEF initiated a project to explore the near- and long-term forces in global financial markets. A first report was published in January 2009 and a further study focusing on selected near-term challenges came out a year later.[68] The long-term view mainly presented in the first publication "The future of the global financial system" is based on scenario thinking.

The WEF conducted a scenario analysis about the future of the global financial system. In this process, more than 250 financial executives, regulators, policy-makers and senior academics attended eight different workshops. The objective was the inclusion of external forces and critical uncertainties with scenario thinking and thus overcome simple extension of current trends. As a result, the outcome should be a support for strategic decision-making.

The study is structured in three chapters. Firstly, the macroeconomic landscape is analysed. Thereafter a near-term industry outlook is given. Finally, the scenario process for the future of the global financial system is outlined. In this section, the authors make extensive use of the opportunity to illustrate the approach and the results.

The scenario process was set up in eight workshops with overall more than 250 experts included. An eight-step scenario approach was chosen (see Figure 3-5), which is in fact quite similar to the one described previously. The main difference is the exclusion of step six (forming wild card scenarios). Instead, the transfer into strategic options and the definition of indicators and signposts is separated in two steps. Both approaches make sense, as the value of extreme scenarios is mainly opening eyes for very uncertain outcomes, which is the aim of this study. However, the definition of signpost and indicators generates a high value-added for readers of the financial market scenarios.

---

[67] WEF (2009b).

[68] WEF (2009a and 2010).

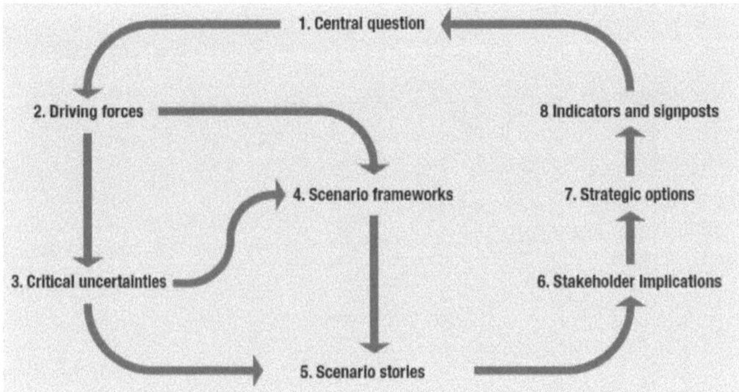

Figure 3-5: Eight-step scenario process applied by WEF[69]

The scenario process is driven by the inputs of the first four steps. The central question in that process is "*How might the governance and structure of the global financial system evolve over both the near-term and long-term*?" Thereafter the key forces regarding this question such as energy prices, global economic growth and energy innovation are defined and categorized in an uncertainty-impact analysis (see Figure 3-6). Finally, the deductive approach of the scenario process requires the selection of the two most critical uncertainties for the global financial system. In the definition of the WEF, these two important critical uncertainties may include several factors shown in the uncertainty-impact matrix and are defined as "pace of geo-economic power shifts" and the "degree of international coordination on financial policy".

[69] According to WEF (2009a).

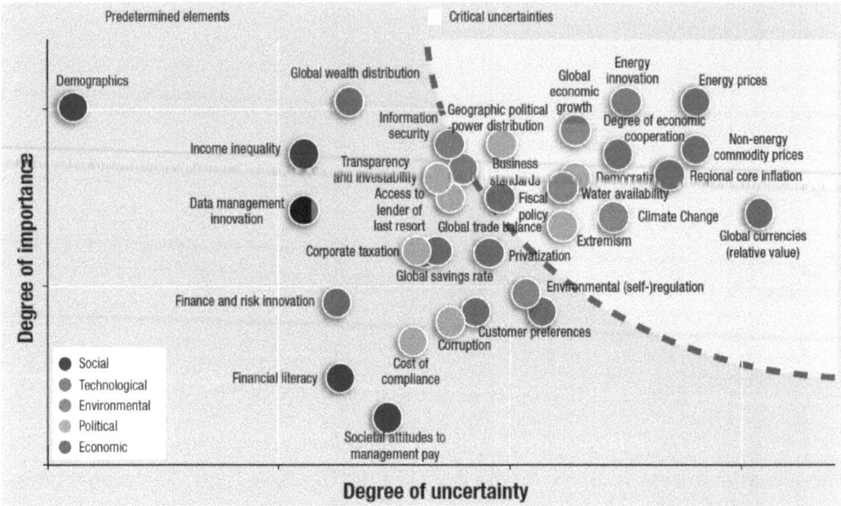

Figure 3-6: Uncertainty-impact analysis of WEF scenario process[70]

The scenario matrix with the axes "pace of geo-economic power shifts" and the "degree of international coordination on financial policy" determines four scenarios. These four scenarios are named "re-engineered western centrism", "rebalanced multilateralism", "fragmented protectionism" and "financial regionalism" (see Figure 3-7). Firstly, in the scenario "re-engineered western centrism" the geo-economic power shift is slow and western countries stay in the focus. Moreover the international financial policy is well coordinated. Secondly, a scenario with a rapid geo-economic power shift until 2020 and a harmonized international financial policy is named "rebalanced multilateralism". Thirdly, the scenario "fragmented protectionism" reveals a discordant coordination of international financial policy combined with a slow power shift in the geo-economy. The final scenario is built in a world of a rapid geo-economic power shift as well as an uncoordinated approach in international financial policy and is named "financial regionalism".

[70] According to WEF (2009a).

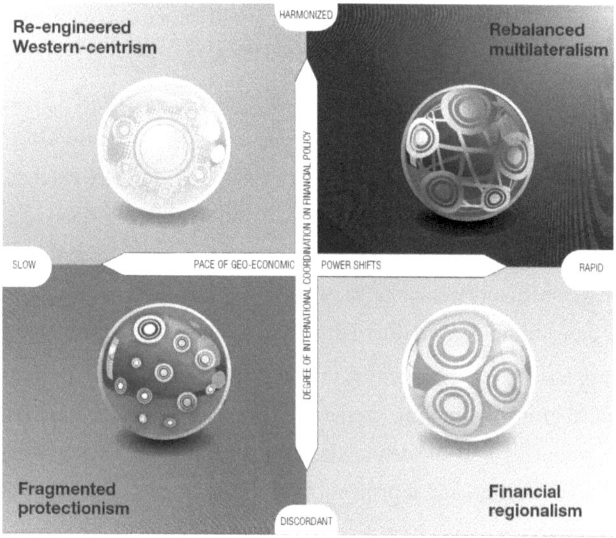

Figure 3-7: Scenario matrix of WEF scenario process[71]

The second half of the scenario process is only briefly commented in the WEF report. This part would be of interest for practitioners as it leads from scenarios to implications. Moreover neither a strategy nor indicators for a monitoring cockpit are outlined in this report; however it is said to be discussed in a further study. Unfortunately the latest WEF study (2010) on the new financial architecture focuses on the near-term and does not pick up the results of the scenario process.

3.4.2 Scenario analysis "European energy security 2020"

Another current example is a study on energy supply in Europe in 2020 authored by the "Stiftung Wissenschaft und Politik" (SWP).[72] The scenario process applied in that case uses a quantitative cross-impact matrix instead of the uncertainty-impact

[71] According to WEF (2009a).

[72] SWP (2008). The German Institute for International and Security Affairs of the *Stiftung Wissenschaft und Politik* (SWP) is an independent scientific establishment that conducts practically oriented research on the basis of which it then advises the *Bundestag* (the German parliament) and the federal government on foreign and security policy issues.

matrix to generate scenarios. However, the overall process is similar even though the tools differ.

The scenario process of the SWP deals with the problem set of "*European energy security in 2020 – a development in Europe and the energy-politically relevant neighbouring areas*". The term neighbouring areas is defined extensively and includes also Russia, Kazakhstan, the Near East and Middle East as well as Northern Africa. Furthermore, two facts are given for the process. Firstly, fossil energy sources will be sufficiently available until 2020. Secondly, other regions become increasingly demanding competitors in the energy market for Europe and the USA.

In a process lasting eleven months, the energy, economic and political experts of SWP formed a group with four scenario experts of Daimler AG. After defining problem set, premises and the team, the brainstorming of 18 key forces (descriptors), a detailed definition and a projection of these factors for 2020 were examined (see Figure 3-8).

Descriptors	Projections	Probability
Joint European energy policy	EU takes the lead	30%
	EU does not take the lead	70%
Stable statehood (producer countries)	pronounced	60%
	restricted	40%
Actors in inner-European market (oil/gas)	undisputed position of traditional actors	60%
	significant influence of new actors	40%
Geopolitical orientation (producer countries)	realignment	30%
	traditional orientation	70%
Wars in the region	conflagration	30%
	isolated conflicts	50%
	no wars	20%
Attractivity of EU as trading partner	decreased	60%
	increased	40%
Demand for imports of fossil energy sources in EU	increased	70%
	stable	20%
	decreased	10%
Multilateral juridification of energy relationships	predominantly yes	30%
	predominantly no	70%
Perception of transnational terrorism	increasing	30%
	level of 2007	50%
	decreasing	20%
Energy as instrument of foreign policy (producer countries)	often applied	40%
	rarely applied	60%
Energy prices	very high oil price ~USD 150	10%
	medium range oil price ~USD 70-90	60%
	low oil price ~USD 25	30%
Development strategies (producer countries)	successful	30%
	unsuccessful	70%
Market power of energy cartel	high/increasing	40%
	low/decreasing	60%
Structure of energy sector (producer countries)	predominantly state-controlled	60%
	hybrid: state and private	30%
	predominantly private sector	10%
US-policy	interventionism	40%
	cooperations	50%
	isolationism	10%
Institutionalized relationship of EU production countries (without energy)	high degree	60%
	low degree	40%
Investments in gas sector	sufficient	60%
	insufficient	40%
Investment in oil sector	high	40%
	low	30%

Figure 3-8: Descriptors and projection in the SWP scenario process[73]

[73] According to SWP (2008).

In the fourth step of the scenario approach, this process differs from the outlined standard methodology. In this case, the scenario experts decided to apply a cross-impact matrix instead of an uncertainty-impact matrix. A cross-impact matrix is generated by quantitative evaluations of the interaction of the eighteen descriptors in each projection (see Figure 3-9). For example, if growth and inflation are two descriptors and have the projections high and low, then the correlation of high inflation and high growth and the other three possible states is analysed. One easily perceives the complexity of this methodology, which is exponentially growing with the number of descriptors and projections. However, a cross-impact matrix allows a quantitative simulation of steady state scenarios. From this process, 42 steady state scenarios resulted.

			Joint European energy policy		Stable statehood (producer countries)		Actors in inner-European market (oil/gas)		Geopolitical orientation (producer countries)		Wars in the region			Attractivity of EU as trading partner		Demand for imports of fossil energy sources in EU		
Descriptors	**Projections**	**Probability**	a	b	a	b	a	b	a	b	a	b	c	a	b	a	b	c
Joint European energy policy	EU takes the lead	30%			0		-2	1	1	0	2	1	0	1	-1	1	0	-1
	EU does not take the lead	70%					2	-1	-1	0	-1	0	0	-1	1	-1	0	1
Stable statehood (producer countries)	pronounced	60%	0				0		0		-3	-1	1	0		0		
	restricted	40%									3	1	-1					
Actors in inner-European market (oil/gas)	undisputed position of traditional actors	60%	0		0				0		1	0	0	0		0		
	significant influence of new actors	40%									-1	0	0					
Geopolitical orientation (producer countries)	realignment	30%	-2	1	0		0				1	0	0	1	-1	0		
	traditional orientation	70%	2	-1							-1	0	0	-1	1			
Wars in the region	conflagration	30%	0		-3	2	0		0					0		0		
	isolated conflicts	50%			-1	3												
	no wars	20%			0	-3												
Attractivity of EU as trading partner	decreased	60%	0		0		0		0		0					-1	0	1
	increased	40%														1	0	-1
Demand for imports of fossil energy sources in EU	increased	70%	0		0		0		0		0			0	1			
	stable	20%												0	0			
	decreased	10%												0	-1			
Multilateral juridification of energy relationships	predominantly yes	30%	3	-1	0	-2	0		-2	0	-3	-1	0	-1	1	0		
	predominantly no	70%	-2	1	0	2			2	0	3	1	0	1	-1			
Perception of transnational terrorism	increasing	30%	0		0	2	0		0		2	1	0	0		0		
	level of 2007	50%			0	1					-1	0	1					
	decreasing	20%			0	-1					-2	-1	0					
Energy as instrument of foreign policy (producers)	often applied	40%	-1	1	0		0	1	2	0	2	3	0	0		0		
	rarely applied	60%	1	-1			0	-1	-2	0	-2	-3	0					

Figure 3-9: Extract of the cross-impact matrix in the SWP scenario process[74]

Out of these 42 steady state scenarios, the process team selected three scenarios, which are described in an extensive scenario story. The three scenarios are named "elusive security", "expensive oil for a united Europe" and "Europe in an energy-

[74] According to SWP (2008).

political offside position". Interested persons are advised to read those very interesting and illustrative scenarios in SWP (2008).

The scenario process group is the main advantage of this scenario methodology in comparison to the WEF process. A platform like the WEF needs to integrate various persons for political reasons, whereas a scenario process is a tool that is especially designed for small groups.[75] These allow intensified discussions with the integration of external experts if needed. Beyond this, a certain group spirit that drives the process and generates excellent and sometimes surprising results is created. The implementation of the quantitative cross-impact matrix approach is a great rarity in scenario thinking as numerous interactions have to be identified and a consensus needs to be reached among the participants. Hence, it is a complex, time-consuming and intensive process that delivers very elaborate scenarios.

3.5 Combining scenario approach and asset allocation

The asset class specific assumptions in an asset allocation process are generally based on different regimes. These regimes are often defined by macroeconomic scenarios. Thus, in several regimes expected return, expected risk and correlation parameters have to be defined (see Figure 3-10). Usually, one overall regime is calculated according to a weighting of the different regimes. Finally, this overall regime is optimized with portfolio theory tools.[76]

[75] Besides, the scenario expert GED DAVIS (2004) designed a methodology that allows scenario groups of more than 60 persons. However, some main advantages of scenario processes such as discussions and the group spirit disappear.

[76] Another approach is an optimization of each regime and a final maximization of the portfolio considering the efficient frontiers of the different regimes and the estimated regime weights.

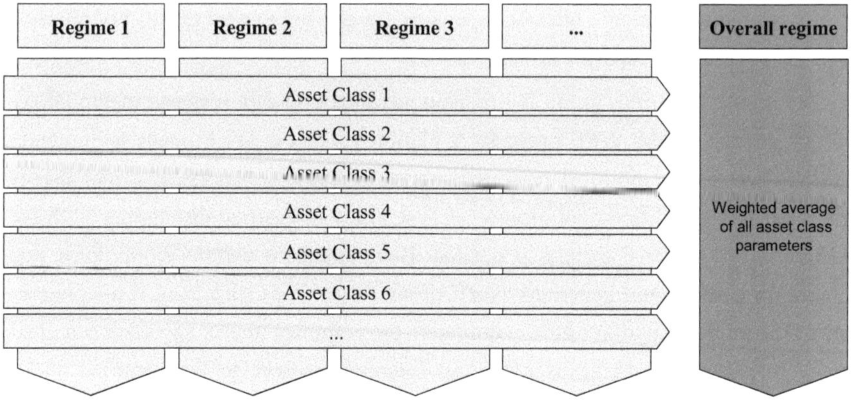

Figure 3-10: Standard asset allocation input parameter framework

The scenario approach and asset allocation processes have several characteristics in common. Both scenario and asset allocation process operate either with scenarios or regimes. In an asset allocation framework the regimes are often defined by macroeconomic conditions and the input parameters for every asset class in these regimes are needed. However, the scenario approach is a strategic tool that defines scenarios in a certain context for example "*how does the global macroeconomic environment develop until 2020*" or more specific "*how will global equity markets develop until 2020*". Transferred into an asset allocation context, question one defines several regimes whereas question two specifically analyses one single asset class. This describes two different approaches integrating scenario methodologies into asset allocation.

A scenario process can help to define the regimes used in an asset allocation framework. As mentioned above, the future global macroeconomic environment can be analysed with a scenario process. Thus, several macroeconomic regimes are defined. Later on, parameters such as expected return, risk and correlation are derived for all considered asset classes.

A second approach to benefit from scenario thinking in asset allocation is analyzing the return, risk and correlation parameters for a specific asset class. In that case, a scenario process for one or even more asset classes is conducted. As a result, several asset class specific scenarios are defined and the required asset allocation parameters are derived. However, the scenarios may not fit to the regimes defined for other asset classes. This leads to a restriction in the asset allocation framework, because it is then required to optimize the weighted averages of all regimes. Due to the fact that this approach generates several different regimes for every single asset class, it is not possible to perform an optimization within each regime and maximize the portfolio with the efficient frontiers of all regimes in a second step. In general, this restriction does not affect portfolio optimization processes in practice as most asset managers focus on optimizing a weighted average of regimes (the overall regime).

Both approaches of integrating scenario methodologies into asset allocation generate advantages. On the one hand, the whole framework of the regimes is defined and specified by comprehensive multidimensional scenarios and not only macroeconomic figures, which are often reduced to a growth and inflation matrix (see Figure 3-11). On the other hand, asset class specific scenarios are defined and asset allocation input parameters derived. This second approach has one major advantage: asset allocation is based on the assumption of diversification effects. If this is true and diversification is not a linear phenomenon, asset classes have and require a different set of scenarios and regimes. For example, catastrophe bonds are said to be almost uncorrelated to financial markets and macroeconomic conditions.[77] However, also for cat bonds several scenarios exist, but these cannot be integrated into a macroeconomic based framework. Therefore, an independent regime structure for some or even every considered asset class creates a competitive advantage in asset allocation. As a consequence, the way of integrating scenario methodologies in asset allocation depends on the objective of the asset allocation. The analysis of every single asset class or at least some asset class categories[78] is the more adequate way. However, up to now asset managers often focus on general macroeconomic regimes.

---

[77] KIELHOLZ & DURRER (1997), p. 11.

[78] The scenarios of some asset classes might overlap, for example equity, investment grade, high yield and convertible bonds.

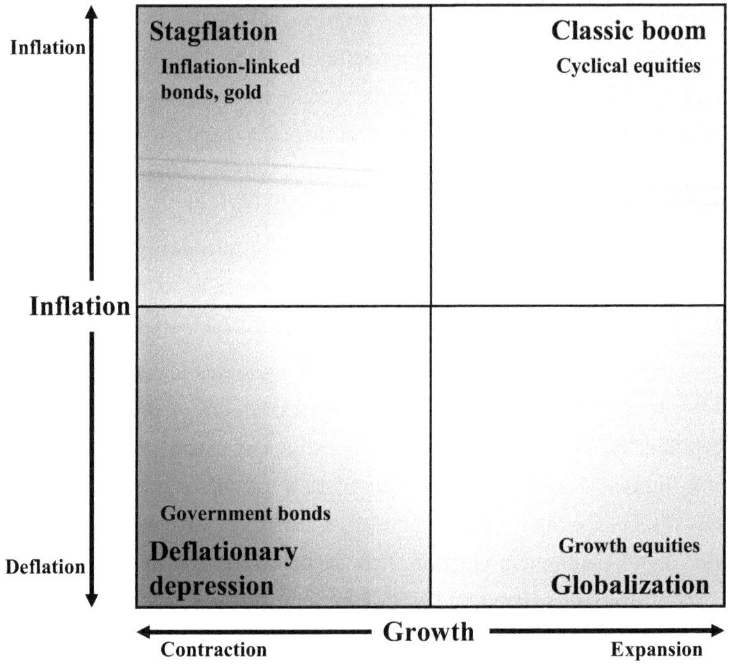

Figure 3-11: Macroeconomic framework for asset allocation

The analysis of asset classes with scenario methodologies provides an innovative tool for asset allocation. This allows generating asset allocation input parameters with asset class specific scenarios. Up to now, asset managers generally rely on macroeconomic regimes that are assumed to be relevant for all asset classes. Moreover, the expectations for return, risk and correlation are derived by a quantitative analysis of the past. For this reason, an economic cycle analysis is performed to determine the parameters by past experiences in similar regimes. More and more experts and investors doubt this forward projection of quantitatively derived past parameters. Furthermore, a clear restriction applies. A considered asset class has to pass through at least one full economic cycle before it can be included in the process. At this point, backward-looking quantitative methods have their limits and forward-looking scenario methodologies may convince not only innovative asset managers.

Scenario methodologies allow an integration of new asset classes. If not sufficient backward-looking data or market values are available, the traditional analysis for asset allocation parameters is limited. The forward-looking qualitative modelling of expected asset class parameters is necessary. Furthermore, asset classes with long-data history can also benefit from a more forward-looking qualitative rather than a backward-looking quantitative process to generate asset allocation input parameters.

The integration of a qualitative process in the quantitatively driven environment of finance may encounter difficulties. On the one hand, process driven problems such as the derivation of quantitative parameters out of qualitative scenarios have to be considered. This is a critical point that has to be addressed, but it can be dealt with.[79] On the other hand, qualitative thinking is not broadly common anymore in various areas of asset allocation. Instead, in recent years practitioners and researchers apply increasingly quantitative methods and tools. Therefore, implementing a qualitative approach of future-oriented research in a quantitative driven environment requires a well-structured and -positioned process to increase acceptance.

3.6 Summary

The scenario approach is a tool to improve long-term strategic decision making. In a scenario process several possible scenarios of the future are generated in a structured assessment. The integration of all relevant factors for a given problem set is a key characteristic. Hence, the methodology is a forward-looking tool that deals with and also structures complexity. As a result, the scenario approach enables qualitative thinking. Furthermore, it provides an innovative tool for dealing with uncertainty and complexity in asset allocation.

[79] GOTTSCHALK & STEINBRECHER (2005) explicitly describe the process of transferring qualitative scenario inputs into a quantitative framework.

4 Microfinance

4.1 Introduction to microfinance

4.1.1 Evolution of microfinance

Microfinance has been a success story over past decades. Nevertheless, core elements of today's microfinance framework have been used for centuries. In Ireland, the author Dean Jonathan Swift initiated entities called "loan funds". These funds accommodated microcredits to entrepreneurs starting in 1720. About one hundred years later, the government established a statutory basis resulting in a boom of "loan funds".[80] A second example is the German "Sparkassen" and cooperative banking system. The first "Sparkasse" was established 1778 in Hamburg. In addition to saving deposits, services included loans for businesses and farmers. In 1846, Friedrich Wilhelm Raiffeisen and Hermann Schulze-Delitzsch founded cooperatives focusing on saving and lending deposits for small businesses and farmers.[81] All three mentioned German banking institutions are major retail banks today: "Sparkassen", "Raiffeisen" and "Volksbanken".

The roots of today's microfinance in emerging markets lie in the mid 1970s.[82] Mohammed Yunus started in 1976 during a famine period to lend money to people of his community. Seven years later, Grameen Bank was founded and Bangladesh became a textbook example for microfinance. During the same period, ACCION in Brazil and Bank Rakyat in Indonesia developed similar microcredit business models. Failed subsidy programmes are one of the major reasons for the popularity of these and other microfinance institutions in emerging markets. Local governments set up rural development programmes financed by development finance institutions (DFIs) such as the World Bank, its private sector affiliate, the International Finance Corporation (IFC) or the German Kreditanstalt für Wiederaufbau (KfW). However, several factors led to a failure of these subsidised development aid programmes.[83] Firstly, local banks were not able to work profitably with the regulated interest

---

[80] HOLLIS & SWEETMAN (1997, 2003) provide a more detailed insight into Irish "loan funds".
[81] SEIBEL (2003, 2005) reveals the roots of microfinance in Germany.
[82] VON PISCHKE (2008), p. 1.
[83] FELDER-KOZU (2008), p. 26.

rates, because operating costs were too high in many regions. Secondly, many debtors considered the loans as donors of their government and hence did neither pay interest rates nor the credit amount at maturity. Thirdly, the rationing of credit programmes fostered corruption in bank lending. Hence, locally originated microfinance proved to be the better solution. It has become one of the rare financial and sustainable success stories of today's emerging and developing markets[84] financial system.

4.1.2 Definitions and categories

Microfinance institutions (MFIs) provide various products for mainly low-income clients mostly in emerging and developing markets.[85] Among those are credits, savings deposits, insurances and pension products.

The main product of microfinance is the microcredit concept. A clear definition and segmentation of the loan and credit segment is crucial. In fact, three main credit types exist in emerging markets (see Figure 4-1). Firstly, consumer credits are used to finance a non-durable good and hence have to be financed by the clients' personal income. Secondly, entrepreneurs can draw on a credit to establish a business or moderately expand an existing one. This kind of credit is referred to as microcredits. The interest payment is generated out of the business' cash flow. Due to the entrepreneurial concept of microcredit, generally no or only insufficient collateralization is possible. Thirdly, corporate credits with adequate collateral exist. This is a common pattern of (small) business lending. As a consequence, the distinction of income-financed consumer credits and cash-flow-financed microcredits is a critical differentiation factor in microfinance.

[84] In the following chapters, the term emerging market is used both for emerging and developing markets. Developing countries are usually nations with a low level of material being such as Honduras, Benin or Bangladesh. Countries considered to be in a transitional phase to developed markets are called emerging markets. Brazil, China, South Africa and Russia are examples for emerging countries.

[85] Common definitions for microfinance can be found on www.microrate.org, www.themix.org or www.responsAbility.org.

Consumer Credit	Microcredit	Small business lending
▪ Credit for non-durable good or consumer durable ▪ Accommodation of a loan shall depend on income	▪ Credit for entrepreneur to establish a business or expand an existing business moderately ▪ Interest payment is generated out of business (→ cash flow calculation necessary) ▪ No (or insufficient) collateralization	▪ Corporate credit ▪ Collateralization

Figure 4-1: Segmentation of credit categories

Microcredits are business loans and by definition not consumer loans. These loans shall support and initiate business concepts, which finance their capital costs out of the business. The clear separation from income-dependent consumer financing enables high repayment rates. However, interest rates are relatively high compared to developed country rates. Firstly, credits are in local currency and therefore refer to local rates. Secondly, clients are widespread and the loan amount is comparably low. Thus, operating costs are on a very high level. Nevertheless, microfinance institutions offer rates which are far below money lender rates.[86]

Savings deposits are a further product and gain importance for microfinance institutions.[87] On the one hand, it is a refinancing option especially in situations when local currency credit markets are limited. On the other hand, it enables MFIs to increase the commitment of their creditors, because these often have savings deposits as well. However, due to regulatory issues MFIs cannot accept deposits in all countries and in general a banking licence is a prerequisite. Also clients can profit from savings deposits, because they get the opportunity to deposit money and get a small interest on the amount. From a western perspective this argument may sound

[86] ROSENBERG ET. AL (2009), p. 20.
[87] MIX (2008), p. 28.

unfamiliar, but in several countries clients would otherwise have to pay a fee for a deposit instead of receiving interest.[88] In conclusion, MFIs as well as clients can profit from savings accounts.

Further products are offered in the segment of microinsurance and -pension.[89] The product range is equally to common insurance and pension products, but contract sizes are very low and operational costs high. Overall, this market is still in an early stage of development. However, in some countries such as Bangladesh with Grameen Bank it is already emerging rapidly. As a result, even major players such as Allianz, Munich Re and Swiss Re have entered this high growth potential market.

4.2 Microfinance market from an investment perspective

4.2.1 Market overview

The microfinance market is structured horizontally along the financial value chain (see Figure 4-2). MFIs grant entrepreneurs a loan with a fixed interest rate in local currency. In the strict sense, the debtor uses the loan to finance an entrepreneurial business and serves the interest payments out of the business' cash flows. In some cases, debtors also have a savings deposit at a MFI with a small or sometimes even no accruing interest. This is one of the main refinancing options for MFIs. Further refinancing includes debt obligations from microfinance investment vehicles (MIVs) or direct investor, local credit markets and equity investments.

[88] CGAP (2007), p. 1.
[89] CHURCHILL (2006), p. 13.

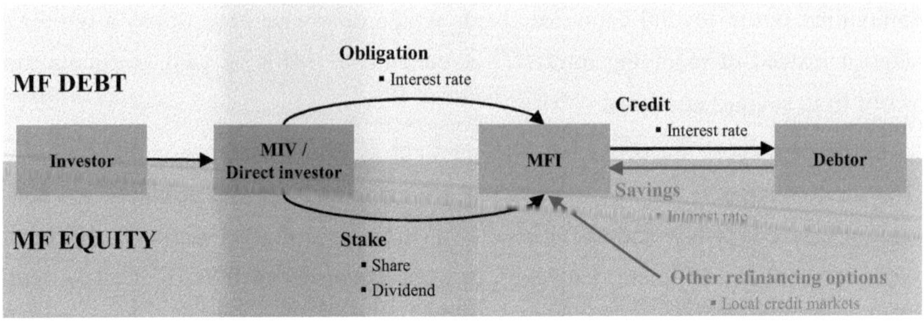

Figure 4-2: Investment perspective on microfinance market

A broad spectrum of service providers complements the microfinance market. Besides the above mentioned market participants of the direct value chain several segments of service providers emerged (see Figure 4-3). The service providers are segmented in three categories. Firstly, DFIs offer technical assistance as well as subsidized funding. Secondly, service providers in a broader sense such as specified data providers, specialised accountants and lawyers as well as FX hedging specialists serve the niche market. Finally, rating agencies complement the microfinance market. These companies either focus on microfinance such as MicroRate or agencies extended their business to microfinance such as Fitch.

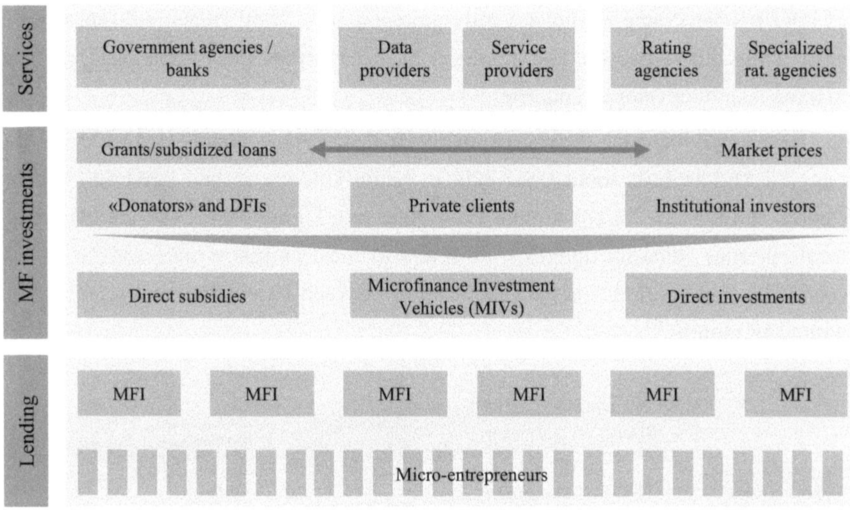

Figure 4-3: Overview of microfinance market

The microfinance market exhibits a mature market structure. However, the market is young and various segments as well as market participants are newly developed or incorporated. Nevertheless, the market is innovative and able to deal with nearly any kind of issue. But in some cases the processes are not defined strictly and mutually agreed procedures are not arranged yet.[90]

4.2.2 Microfinance users

The typical microfinance user is a debtor and client of a MFI.[91] Generally, the person is to some extent a micro-entrepreneur working as a street vendor, farmer, fisherman, salesman, or service provider. Microfinance clients are also often described according to their poverty level. However, the idea of microfinance is not donating for the poor. In fact, it is enabling and supporting the entrepreneurial spirit

[90] One example is the provisioning policy of MIVs during 2009. Whereas some funds made provisions for a debt obligation to a specific MFI, other funds with the same exposure did not. However, the industry leaders will figure out a common provisioning procedure.

[91] In this and the following chapters, the term microfinance is used in a broader context even though the focus is often on the microcredit segment.

of poor people. Some clients are truly entrepreneurs. They create and run a business, while others became entrepreneurs by necessity as the formal sector is less marked than in developed countries.

The average loan size differs regionally: in Asia approximately USD 200, in Africa and Middle East about USD 300, in Latin America around USD 800 and in Central and Eastern Europe around USD 2000 (see Figure 4-4).[92] The credits are in local currency, thus the interest rate refers to local currency rates and operating costs. The credit period is in the vast majority between 12 and 36 months, averaging around 18 months.[93]

	Africa	Asia	Eastern Europe & Central Asia	Latin America & the Caribbean	Middle East & Northern Africa
% of women	57.2	93.8	43.1	59.6	65.4
Average loan (in USD)	308	166	2174	780	317
Average deposit (in USD)	98	56	1855	466	26

Figure 4-4: Some key figures of microfinance users[94]

The gender is a further important criterion in the microfinance segment. Overall, roughly 60% of the credits are allowed to women.[95] Furthermore, in some areas in Asia and Africa group lending is preferred as it generates social control. Another rarely stated reason for the group lending phenomenon is the loan amount. In Eastern Europe loans are on average roughly ten times higher than in Asia and therefore operating costs are assumed to be lower, which makes individual lending more

[92] MIX (2009), p. 48. A normalization of the average loan size by a factor such as GDP per capita would bring the outstanding amount in Eastern Europe & Central Asia closer to the average.
[93] MIX (2008) and information from www.themix.org
[94] According to MIX (2009).
[95] MIX (2009), p. 48.

profitable than for example in Asia.[96] This might be another factor allowing individual lending, besides the often stated cultural and social differences.[97]

4.2.3 Microfinance institutions

MFIs are organizations offering microcredits and in some cases savings accounts. Hence, the balance sheet assets are credits allowed to micro-entrepreneurs. The liability structure depends on the MFI's refinancing strategy, corporate status and regulatory issues (see Figure 4-5).[98] Adequate financing sources are equity, international capital markets, local capital markets, deposit accounts and subsidies such as supranational funding or even donations.

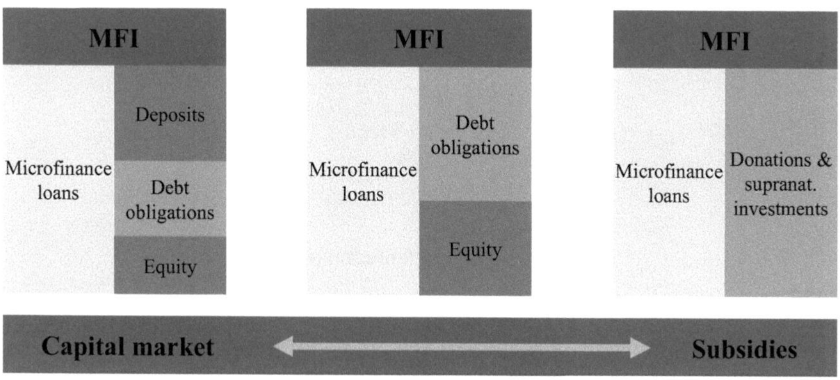

Figure 4-5: Lending and funding strategies of MFIs

The refinancing strategy of MFIs is dependent on their development stage. Mature and well-known MFIs are clustered as Tier 1. These institutions are in the majority of the cases banks, regulated by a governmental authority and also covered by rat-

[96] Again, the local compensation levels have to be taken into account. These are higher in most countries of Eastern Europe compared to other emerging markets.

[97] The argument of is supported by data of the MBB 19 (MIX 2009). The PAR30 for solidarity lending (1.5%) was in 2008 markedly below individual lending (3.4%). However, the profit margin for these solidarity loans were slightly negative (-0.7%), whereas for individual loans a profit of 7.3% arose. The different average loan size of USD 111 for group lending as opposed to USD 1404 for individual lending might give an explanation.

[98] DIECKMANN (2007), p. 6.

ing agencies. Tier 2 MFIs are smaller and not all processes are perfectly structured yet. However, these institutes are candidates for a conversion into banks. The third group and majority of MFIs are NGOs or start-ups. These organizations are mostly unprofitable and often follow exclusively social objectives. As a result, MFIs can be clustered into a pyramid scheme (see Figure 4-6) with only a few mature institutions. Nevertheless, these Tier 1 and 2 MFIs grant about 90% of the loan sum.[99]

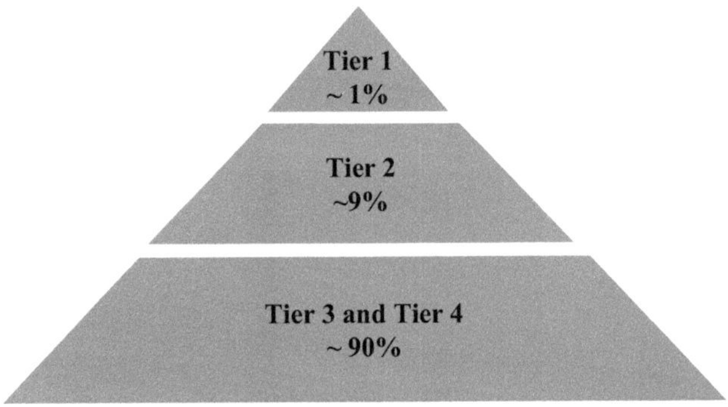

Figure 4-6: Segmentation of MFIs

Microfinance investment vehicles (MIVs), local banks, development agencies, donators and international credit markets facilitate the refinancing of MFIs. The mature MFIs have access to local capital markets as well as investment funds to leverage their equity. Furthermore, these institutions generally have a banking license and consequently accept deposits as further refinancing facility. For these reasons, mature MFIs are able to lever their equity up to seven times.[100] The average debt to equity multiple of Tier 1 and 2 MFIs is about three.[101] However, the majority of MFIs operates less professional and refinances the microcredits with loans from development agencies or donations.

[99] MIX (2009), p. 47.
[100] HUBER (2009).
[101] MIX (2009), p. 47.

The outstanding loan portfolio of about 1000 major MFIs was about USD 40 billion according to TheMix database.[102] Indeed, these data are not exclusively based on microcredits, but also contain consumer lending and small business lending. An amount of about USD 30 billion seems more adequate according to estimates of various microfinance experts from MicroRate or responsAbility.[103] These credits are funded by savings deposits, donations, paid in capital and borrowings.[104]

MFIs require local currency refinancing with matching maturities to their credits. But international investors such as investment funds or even governmental investments prefer hard currency debt obligations. Accordingly, the MFI or the debtor would have to dare the currency risk. In case of strong currency devaluation, the risk taker could default.[105] Thus, MFI and investor assign a reliable counterparty for foreign exchange risks. In some countries, the international capital market offers derivative instruments such as non-deliverable forwards. In the vast majority of cases, currency hedging can only be provided by local banks that take the risk for high premiums. Overall, the foreign exchange risk for international investors such as development agencies and MIVs has gained importance over the last years.[106]

The refinancing structure of MFIs is dominated by local sources. Savings accounts of microfinance clients make up on average 45% of the balance sheet. Additionally, roughly 30% are refinanced with domestic credit lines or equity investments. Hence, less than 25% are financed by foreign investors (see Figure 4-7). However, this still amounts to about USD 7.5 billion financed from foreign sources such as MIVs and direct investments.

---

[102] See figure prominently displayed at www.mixmarket.com.
[103] Interviews with Damian von Stauffenberg and Patrik Huber.
[104] Estimate considering MIX (2008), p. 26 and current data available on www.themix.org indicating a gross loan portfolio of roughly USD 40 billion. However, these figures do not exclusively focus on microcredits, but also contain consumer lending and some small business lending. Hence a discount factor of 25% adjusts for the data inconsistency. This discount factor was intensively discussed was experts from MicroRate and responsAbility.
[105] In some central Asian countries this "hedging" approach was implemented and consequently the client was opposed to the currency risk. As a result, the market was hit hard during the financial crisis. From now on, a better hedging approach is considered.
[106] HUBER (2009).

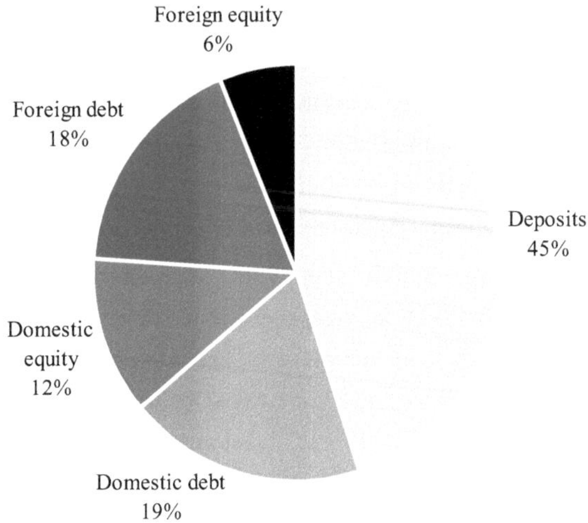

Figure 4-7: Refinancing structure of MFIs[107]

The funding structure of MFIs differs regionally. Interestingly, the refinancing gap with respect to deposits is highest in Asia (see Figure 4-8). In the other three main regions, roughly 50% of the loans are funded by deposits. However, the data quality regarding microfinance is rather poor.[108] As a result, the tapping of various different refinancing sources especially client deposits requires a sound asset liability management for MFIs and is critical to assess and manage financial risks.[109]

107 MCKINSEY (2006), DIECKMANN (2007) and discussed with microfinance experts of MicroRate and responsAbility.

108 Data ascertainment is difficult for several reasons such as definition of microcredit, data processing technology, and exchange rate fluctuation.

109 For a detailed insight in asset liability management of MFIs refer to CGAP (2009c).

	Africa	Asia	Eastern Europe & Central Asia	Latin America & the Caribbean	Middle East & Northern Africa
Offices (in '000)	4	23	3	9	2
Employees (in '000)	35	200	39	77	16
Borrowers (in '000)	5'183	43'294	2'387	11'374	2'244
Depositors (in '000)	8'036	11'769	3'891	9'816	9
Loan portfolio (in USD mn)	2'419	6'744	7'776	13'820	1'040
Deposits (in USD mn)	1'948	1'163	3'296	8'637	55

Figure 4-8: The scale of global microfinance institutions[110]

4.2.4 Microfinance investment vehicles

Microfinance investment vehicles are funds or structured products that provide debt obligations to or take equity stakes in MFIs. In general, institutional and private investors have three channels to participate in the microfinance market. Firstly, they can invest directly in business projects of micro-entrepreneurs. Secondly, direct investments can be allocated to MFIs that accommodate a broad range of micro-credits with a regional focus. Finally, investors can place money with MIVs that allocate their portfolio to a diverse range of MFIs.

Direct investments in a single project or a regionally based MFI may generate a high social impact, but also increase risks. Arguments such as regional diversification, selection skills and access to the market are a clear advice to fund investments. However, philantrophic investors and donators prefer the direct contact to their projects.

Microfinance investment vehicles are an increasingly important funding instrument of MFIs. In 2007, MIVs accounted for about USD 4 billion of credit lines and equity investments.[111] In 2009, the boom in microfinance investments slowed down.

---

[110] According to MIX (2008), p. 26. These data exclude Bank Rakyat Indonesia (BRI) with an outstanding volume of microfinance credits of about USD 6 billion.

[111] VON STAUFFENBERG (2008), p. 15.

However, MIVs funding capacity increased also during the credit crises by about 30% per year. Especially governmental vehicles and private investors ensured money inflows. For this reason, MIVS currently have a refinancing capacity of approximately USD 6.5 billion.[112]

Microfinance investment vehicles have different approaches. Firstly, pure microfinance debt obligation funds exist. They often offer a return of Libor plus 200 basis points and charge around 2% management fees. The debt obligations have a maturity of 12 to 36 months and are widely diversified across regions. Secondly, some microfinance equity funds invest directly in equity stages of MFIs. These funds are set up like private equity funds with similar return expectations and fee structures. Thirdly, there are funds combining debt obligations with some equity exposure. Finally, structured vehicles have been set up. These credit loan obligations (CLOs) are less regulated, have a fixed maturity and offer no liquidity. From an investment perspective, these structures are not advisable as the whole investment is placed in one maturity and time horizon. However, long maturities of the debt obligations offer a premium.

A further distinction criterion of microfinance investment vehicles is the foreign exchange approach. Almost every MIV purely invests in hard currency debt obligation, despite the high costs for foreign exchange hedging. However, as investors get more and more experienced this might change in the future and local currency investments will increase.

Some MIVs do not allocate purely to microfinance investments. There are two major reasons for this. Firstly, raised capital cannot be invested at short notice. In the past, MFIs have often aligned the lending policy to the availability of refinancing opportunities. The allowance of credits takes a while and currently the credit crisis also slowed down the need for microcredits. Secondly, cash or liquid assets enhance liquidity options of the fund. In case of withdrawals, the fund cannot liquidate debt obligations as no secondary market exists. A strict asset liability management is crucial. However, interest payments and the short maturity of the debt obligations (on average about 18 months) lead to a constant cash flow. But

---

[112] CGAP (2009b).

reinvestments have to be arranged well in advance in the illiquid microfinance market environment. In conclusion, cash management is a major challenge for MIVs and hence some invest a smaller portion in other more liquid investments.

The market for microfinance investments shows strong and sustained growth. Every other month, a new investment vehicle is launched. In most cases, the vehicles are managed by one of the three big market players BlueOrchard, responsAbility or Symbiotics and only distributed by a new market member. Besides, the debt obligations market for MFIs is a person's business. For example, a general market platform for debt obligations does not exist and access to brokers is limited. Hence, market entry is complicated and only a few companies have the skills and contacts to act successfully including the above mentioned as well as Developing World Markets and Triodos. Overall, about 100 MIVs with investment strategies ranging from pure debt to equity investment exist.[113] The most prominent ones are listed below (see Figure 4-9).

[113] CGAP (2009b) and www.mixmarket.com.

Fund name	Fund manager	Assets allocated to MF, USD mn	Total fund assets, in USD mn	Inception year	Type of fund	Data as of
EFSE (Eur. Fund for Southeast E.)	Oppenheim / KfW	622.6	946.4	2005	Fund - institutionals	Sep 09
Dexia Microcredit Fund	BlueOrchard	384.4	541.7	1998	Fund; pure debt	Dez 09
ResponsAbility Global MF Fund	ResponsAbility	342.2	477.2	2003	Fund - priv.; up tp 10% equity	Jan 10
ResponsAbility MF Leaders Fund	ResponsAbility	133.5	159.7	2006	Fund - inst.; up to 25% equity	Jan 10
ResponsAbility Mikrofinanz-Fonds	ResponsAbility	102.9	143.1	2006	Fund - inst.; pure debt	Jan 10
Dual Return Fund - Vision MF	Symbiotics	94.5	118.2	2006	Fund - private and inst.	Jan 10
Triodos Microfinance Fund	Triodos	30.0	55.0	2009	Fund - private and inst.	Dez 09
Wallberg Global MF	Symbiotics	28.9	39.4	2008	Fund - private and inst.	Dez 09
Enabling Microfinance	Symbiotics	26.0	35.1	2008	Fund - private and inst.	Jan 10
DWM	DWM	7.4	8.5	2009	Fund; up to 50% local FX	Dez 09
SNS Institutional Fund	Triple Jump	195.0	220.0	2007	Closed mutual fund	Sep 08
BlueOrchard Loans for Devel. 2	BlueOrchard	110.0	110.0	2007	CLO - 5 years	Jan 10
BlueOrchard Loans for Devel. 1	BlueOrchard	96.6	99.1	2006	CLO - 5 years	Jan 10
db Microfinance Invest No. 1	Deutsche Bank	87.0	87.0	2004	CLO - 7 years	Jan 10
BlueOrchard MF Securities 1	BlueOrchard	74.0	79.3	2004	CDO - 7 years	Jan 10
ASN Novib Fund	Triple Jump	49.0	84.0	1998	Investment fund	Dez 07
Microfinance Growth Facility	BlueOrchard			2010	USA, target USD 250 mn	Jan 10
Microfinance Enhancement Facility	BO, rA, Cyrano	87.5	122.1	2009	IFC/KfW, target USD 150 mn	Nov 09
Oikocredit		304.9	614.5	1975	Inv. cooperative	Dez 07
ProCredit Holding		296.8			Holding company of MFIs	Dez 08

Figure 4-9: Overview of prominent MIVs[114]

The DFIs and government authorities have implemented two additional MIVs in the aftermaths of the credit crisis. The IFC (the Worldbanks' private investment arm International Finance Corporation) and the KfW (the German Kreditanstalt für Wiederaufbau) set up the microfinance growth facility, which initially had a target size of USD 500 million. However, the refinancing demand of MFIs was vastly overestimated and the target size will be reduced. The US government introduced the so-called "Obama fund", a microfinance growth facility targeting South American funding needs with up to USD 250 million over the next years. These two vehicles will be major market players over the next years and clearly express the motivation of governments to support the microfinance sector.

4.2.5 Microfinance service providers

A wide range of service providers emerges in the environment of the microfinance sector. As mentioned above, these service providers can be categorized in govern-

[114] Data as documented in fund fact sheets or company prospects.

mental services, a wide range of corporate service providers and rating agencies (see Figure 4-3).

Supranational and governmental organization offer technical assistance in the microfinance sector. This includes diagnostics, development of new products and services, implementation of balanced scorecard methods, design of market research strategies, social impact studies, strategic business planning as well as audits.

The corporate service providers are often niche players and have at least a special unit covering microfinance. In portfolio management, accountants and lawyers play a specific role. It starts with the launch of a fund, the valuation, the proof of contracts and many more issues. In Europe, Switzerland and Luxembourg have become the microfinance platforms and the major accounting companies offer specific microfinance services as well as lawyers. Furthermore, brokerage platforms are needed even in microfinance. The major asset managers also cover this at least partially (e.g. Symbiotics, responsAbility). However, also specialized brokers exist. Moreover, data and information platforms such as TheMix or CGAP offer essential value for the microfinance market as a whole.

Service and consulting companies also exist in specific niches. The most prominent business areas for microfinance consulting services are IT solutions and foreign exchange hedging. Obviously, general market research and social impact studies are also major fields.

In microfinance rating agencies exist accordingly to other financial market segments. International and regional rating agencies focusing on microfinance are established and add to the service provided by standard ones. The service mainly includes rating MFIs and tranches of structured vehicles. The market for MFI ratings is segmented. Besides the standard rating agencies, several microfinance specialists such as MicroRate, PlaNet Rating or Microfinanza Rating exist. These often have a regional focus and of course local offices. Hence, they are very much into the business and have close contacts to the local MFIs. Fitch, Standard & Poor's or Moody's additionally offer ratings for structured vehicles. In microfinance, rating agencies charge relatively low or no fees for their rating. However, the rating agencies offer more detailed services to asset managers and investors against charge.

All these services are key elements to provide investment solutions for institutional and private clients in MIVs.[115] In a growing market environment, the service segment will become more specialised and the already high quality standards will improve even more.

4.3 Market situation

4.3.1 Current market conditions

From an investor's perspective, the analysis of market conditions becomes interesting by adding current figures to the key factors. Certainly, an investor can assess the attractiveness of a microfinance investment. Figure 4-10 gives a detailed insight and presents recent data[116] of the invested portfolio of responsAbility Social Investment AG, which are also in line with Microrate's data for major MFIs. The market analysis is looked at from three different points of view: the microcredit debtor, the MFI allowing the credit, and the MIV as one of the funding sources of MFIs.

[115] VON STAUFFENBERG (2008).

[116] Data as of July 2009.

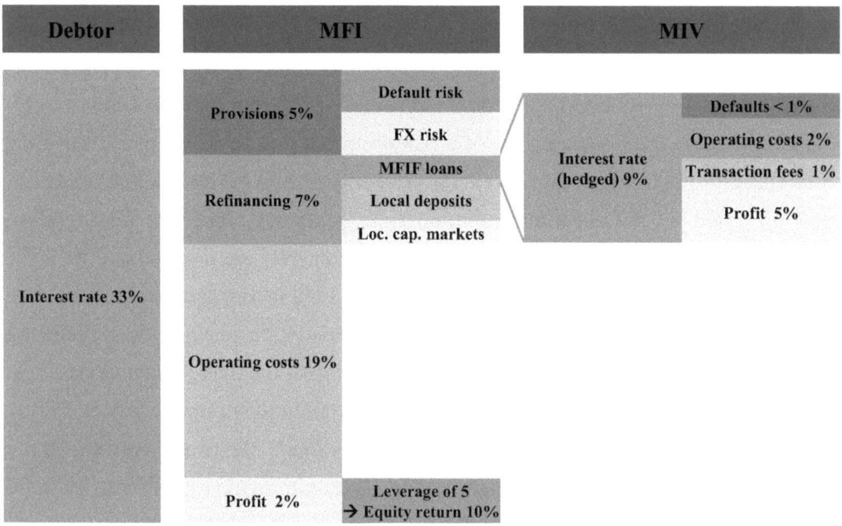

Figure 4-10: Current market conditions in microfinance market

The main player in the cost structure analysis of the microfinance market is the MFI. The MFI has to finance four main positions. Firstly, on average a mature MFI has operating costs of about 19% of the credit amount. The operating costs include the credit agents, accountants, lawyers, regulator fees, and overheads. The operating costs differ regionally. In some areas operating costs of more than 50% apply, for example in Mexico.[117] Secondly, the funding sources for the credit have to be financed. The refinancing costs for a mature MFI are on average 7%. This cost position can be divided in the cost for different funding sources such as MIV loans, local deposits, and local capital market credit lines. Thirdly, a MFI makes provisions for default and foreign exchange risk. Both factors are extremely market driven and vary widely across MFIs. Finally, in general mature MFIs shall generate a return for equity investors. However, as in any other business the profit margin depends on the success of the underlying business. If the MFI follows the golden rules for banks of "matching maturities" and operating costs that are fixed, the only

[117] According to online database of www.mixmarket.org.

uncertainty for profits are provisions such as defaults and other risks. In fact, in the last year provisions increased and profits declined.

Debtors have to pay on average an interest rate of 33% for a microcredit. The interest rate for microcredits consists of a risk premium, the cost of capital, operating costs and a profit margin. These criteria are congruent to credit markets in developed countries yet the costs and premiums are generally higher for microcredits. These four main cost positions for MFIs add to an average interest rate of 33%. Again, the regional differences range from about 15% in Bangladesh to more than 75% in Mexico. Nevertheless, a microcredit is always far cheaper than financing opportunities with "local dealers". In most of the cases, the debtor finances the cost of capital out of generated cash flows. Hence, the credit agent needs a clear picture of the business model of the entrepreneur to evaluate the creditworthiness. Of course this credit assessment is influenced by economic market conditions as these effect business models of entrepreneurs. Consequently, the high cost for microcredits have to be charged with relatively high interest rates.

The insight in the cost analysis of microfinance investment funds is crucial for investors. On the one hand, a market-driven average interest rate for microfinance debt obligations is given. This return component is dependent on demand and supply, but also has a social component as neither DFIs nor MIVs push interest rates to the limit. Additionally, DFIs may also set a price level with subsidized loans. It is essential to internalize, that the interest rates of the debt obligations are not free market rates and may not compensate all risks at any time. Currently, the market has a tremendous supply overhang, because of an increasing MIV volume and new DFI vehicles. The results are decreasing interest rates and also high cash levels in MIVs. On the other hand, operating expenses and provisions of the MIV are the cost. The operating expenses include costs for fund analysis, asset management, sales, and overheads and are charged as a more or less fixed percentage. Moreover, transaction costs such as accountant and lawyer fees, transaction fees and foreign exchange hedging costs are charged against the fund value. Finally, provisions for default risks have to be taken into account. Again, during 2009 some MIVs made the first provisions in microfinance at all. However, up to now all debt obligations and interest rate payments were successfully fulfilled. As a result, the profit for investors in 2009 is lower than in previous years due to decreasing interest rates and some provisions.

The MIVs operating costs and transaction fees are essential for the performance of microfinance investments. The interest rate is more or less fixed due to market conditions and social investment criteria. Hence, the cost structure of the investment vehicle has a huge impact on performance.

4.3.2 Impact of financial crisis

The microfinance market is captured by the phenomenon of the financial crisis. The impact of the financial crisis affects micro-entrepreneurs, MFIs as well as MIVs.

Microfinance clients experienced two major concerns during the financial crisis. In the beginning of the financial crisis, the commodity prices surged and peaked in summer 2008. The result was a dramatic food and energy price inflation. As one might expect, in low-income households in emerging countries these two goods are the main cost factors and non-substitutable goods. As a consequence, operating costs of businesses with energy consumption rose and some microcredits were also partially used to buy comestibles such as rice. The long-term impact of the latter, understandable action is problematic as the microcredit has then to be financed from a lower capital base.

In a second stage of the financial crisis, the emerging markets were hit by an economic downturn. This affected various business models of micro-entrepreneurs, manufacturing, petty trading and agriculture are said to be the sectors hit most severely. The enormous cycle seen in commodity prices and economic growth will have long-term impact on microfinance clients. The payment of interest rates out of cash flows is in several business segments problematic, the repayment of loans in the current stage is critical. However, the impact of the financial crisis and its economic effects differ regionally.

The MFIs experienced the financial crisis on both sides of the balance sheet. Regarding the assets, in most countries clients were affected by economic factors. In some areas, also political and social problems emerged with Nicaragua being an extreme example.[118] In such an environment, the MFIs were obliged to focus on quality instead of quantity. In the aftermath of Lehman, most institutions decided after several years with loan portfolios growing on average with more than 30% to come to a hold. In 2009, the loan portfolios showed nearly no growth in most regions and MFIs.[119] This encouraged MFIs to focus on improving processes such as the credit assessment and risk management, advancing the business model and training the employees. However, the true portfolio risks of MFIs evoked. During the long phase with enormous growth rates, maturing credits were generally prolonged and in most cases extended. As maturing microcredits were generally not increased and in some cases even reduced, it was the first time that in some cases clients had to show willingness and ability of loan repayments.[120] As a result of all these factors, an increasing rate of payments for either interest or loan defaulted. MFIs measure defaults and write-offs with the indicators PAR30 (the portfolio at risk with payments more than 30 days defaulted) and finally the write-offs (see Figure 4-11).

[118] Besides various problems in the Nicaraguan microfinance sector such as weak credit assessments and almost no diversification (most clients do business related to the meat production segment), the Nicaraguan president proclaimed in July 2008 to breach debt contracts and stop payments to microfinance institutions.
[119] CGAP (2009a).
[120] LITTLEFIELD & KNEIDING (2009), p. 4.

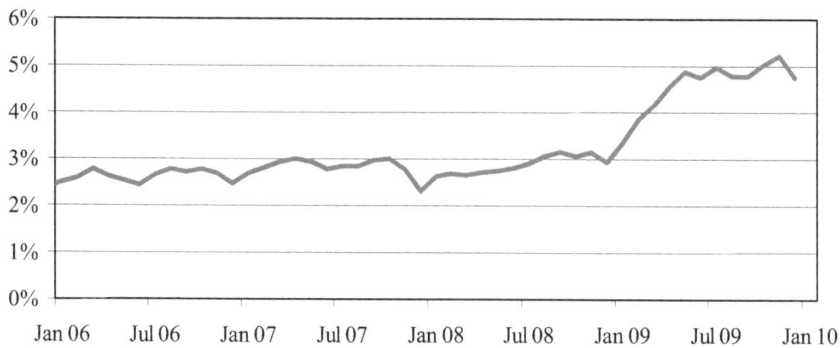

Figure 4-11: PAR30 of Symbiotics50 microfinance index[121]

Furthermore, the international capital markets affected the funding sources of the MFIs. In a first stage, the volatility of foreign exchange markets clearly evoked any hedging issues of MFIs. Simultaneously, at the peak of the financial melt down in October 2008, the most prominent DFIs and MIVs decided to follow a path of cautious growth for the first time. Moreover, local and international capital markets suffered a liquidity shock. As a result, MFIs were forced to change their strategy from growth to value-driven portfolios. In the later stage of the financial crisis, the international capital markets were and still are flooded with liquidity enabling a supply shock of funding sources for MFIs. Hence, MFIs can now profit from low cost of capital and compensate higher defaults to some extent – equal to the situation on developed markets.

The MIVs are trapped by the success of microfinance. During the crisis, microfinance investments were one of the rare asset classes always contributing positive returns. As a matter of fact, in the financial market sell-off and liquidity crisis after Lehman, some major investors had to rebalance portfolios. Thus, there was a short phase in which MIVs had very low or even negative cash positions. On the contrary, the excellent performance generated stable inflows in microfinance funds during 2009. However, the MFIs did not increase their loan portfolio and international markets were flooded with liquidity. On top of that, the Microfinance

---

[121] SYMBIOTICS (2010). The Symbiotics50 index represents data of 50 major MFIs.

Enhancement Facility which was introduced on the peak of the crisis from the two development agencies IFC and KfW started to invest their immense funding capacities of up to USD 500 million. This amount was now reduced and may not exceed USD 130 million, but another Microfinance Growth Facility from the USA will start investing in 2010 (target size USD 250 million). In fact, both funds have a bad timing. Currently, MIVs suffer due to the supply shock and some have cash levels of up to 40%. The DFIs rescue funds decrease interest rates for debt obligations of MFIs and furthermore, the high cash levels harm returns and track record of MIVs. Hence, the private and institutional investors' huge interests as well as the bad timing of political interventions distort the competition.

The financial crisis was the first shock for the microfinance industry and its processes. In general, the very young microfinance industry survived the financial and liquidity crisis quite astonishingly in a sound condition. Many processes worked out, others were adapted quickly. However, some issues such as credit quality, consumer lending and an overhang of liquidity supply of MIVs still exist and will challenge the microfinance industry. Furthermore, in some cases an industry standard is still missing. The provisioning process of MIVs is one example. Even though most funds have investments in the same MFIs, the funds interpret the guidelines for provisioning differently. In the work out case of a Nicaraguan MFI, all major players of the microfinance industry had a shared interest in solving the issue. Nevertheless, the provisioning policies differed across the MIVs. In conclusion, the microfinance industry is challenged by the financial crisis, but it is also an opportunity to demonstrate the capacity and finally become a mature asset class.

4.3.3 Market potential

The microfinance sector has an estimated volume of more than USD 30 billion.[122] However, studies estimate that only 10-15% of micro-entrepreneurs have access to basic financial services. Hence, the potential for microfinance credits is estimated to

[122] See footnote 100.

be around USD 280 billion resulting in an untapped client potential of about USD 250 billion (see Figure 4-12).[123]

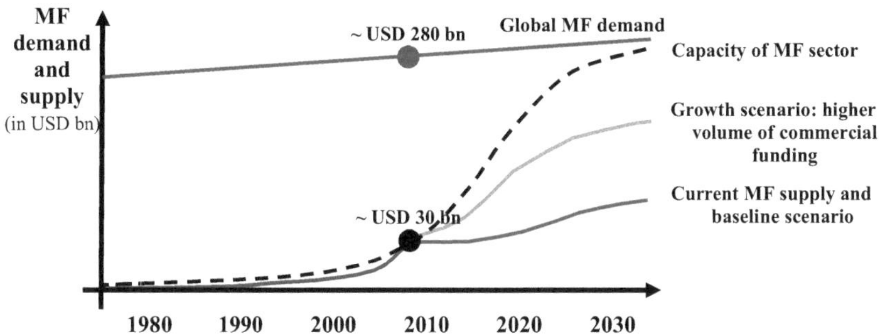

Figure 4-12: The potential of microfinance

The role of international capital markets is crucial to enable the outlined market growth. The funding of microcredits also depends on credit lines. In some countries, MFIs are not allowed to take savings. In addition to that, a banking license including an organisational and regulatory framework is a prerequisite in most countries. Therefore, some MFIs have to rely on MIVs debt obligation and local market credit lines as main funding sources. In addition, also MFIs with a banking license tap international and local credit markets to enable growth. Hence, the potential funding needs from MIVs for the microcredit market can be calculated assuming the present funding structure of MFIs (see Figure 4-7). Currently, foreign capital accounts for more than 20% of the MFIs' funding sources. In conclusion, this would imply a potential funding gap for the international capital markets of more than USD 50 billion.

The acceleration of funding sources during the last few years enabled strong growth in microfinance, which is currently halted due to financial crisis effects. If the economic and financial market situation stabilizes, the success story could pro-

[123] MEEHAN (2004), p 5. The same figures are also stated by many others such as MCKINSEY (2006) and DIECKMANN (2007).

ceed. The prerequisites in form of capacities in various fields of the microfinance sector are provided. Furthermore, the current supply overhang in funding of MFIs would allow a higher growth scenario. However, one risk scenario may include disappointed investors. The high cash levels of MIVs and the decreasing interest rates for debt obligations to MFIs lead to decreasing MIV performances. As a result, the capital might be withdrawn for higher return investments exactly when funding needs return. However, the majority of the investors is not excessively focussed on financial return. As a result, the growth of the microfinance market is dependent on the demand of people in the emerging markets for financial solutions and the capacity of funding sources.

4.4 Microfinance investments – insights and quantitative analysis

4.4.1 Dexia Microcredit Fund

The Dexia Microcredit Fund (DMF) is the public fund with the longest track record. The fund started in 1998 and is managed by the microfinance specialist BlueOrchard. In December 2009, the net asset value (NAV) was USD 542 million. The DMF is one of the most prominent and the largest public microfinance investment vehicle.

The fund invests in debt instruments issued by microfinance institutions with up to three years in maturity. Investments are allocated to MFIs in Africa, Asia, Eastern and Central Europe as well as Latin America. The DMF seeks to achieve an attractive financial return for investors while also providing social impact. The target annual return of the fund is 6-months Libor plus 1-2%.[124] Consequently, the BlueOrchard specialists hedge the interest rate risk of the debt obligations according to the maturity of its benchmark.

The main return characteristics of the DMF are shown in Figure 4-13. The annualised return of the USD tranche was 4.71% since inception and the fund has a

[124] BLUEORCHARD (2009), p. 2.

Sharpe ratio of 1.78.[125] The outstanding Sharpe ratio is caused by the low volatility of the monthly returns.[126]

Investment period	12/1998-02/2010
Return	4.68%
Risk	1.03%
Risk free rate (during period)	2.85%
Sharpe Ratio	1.78

Figure 4-13: Key figures Dexia Microcredit Fund[127]

The correlation matrix with all major asset classes reveals further interesting characteristics (see Figure 4-15). In the overall investment period, the DMF was uncorrelated to many asset classes. Despite a positive correlation to USD money market (0.34) and a negative correlation to commodities (-0.18), the funds correlation was below 0.1 to all other major asset classes. Furthermore, a 12-months rolling correlation analysis approves the comparably low correlation. Moreover microfinance investments have no stable correlation with equity, bond or money market investments (see Figure 4-14). Thus, the often proclaimed low correlation of microfinance can be evidenced by quantitative analysis of fund data. However, the key question is whether the low volatility of the NAV unveils the risks of microfinance investments.

---

[125] The Sharpe ratios are calculated with the returns of 3-months US Treasury bills. Until 2007, the use of the USD 3-months LIBOR would have been adequate. However, the financial crises added very volatile counterparty premiums in the interbank market. As a result, LIBOR rates are not an adequate data series for risk free rates anymore.

[126] The Sharpe ratio is often used in portfolio management and also cited for microfinance. This is the reason, why it is stated here. However, the main problem in measuring microfinance performance adequately is the risk factor. If the risk is underestimated, the Sharpe ratio will be constantly overestimated. In fact, this is exactly the case in microfinance, if risk is measured by fund volatility (for a more detailed discussion see chapter 4.4).

[127] Bloomberg data as of February 2010.

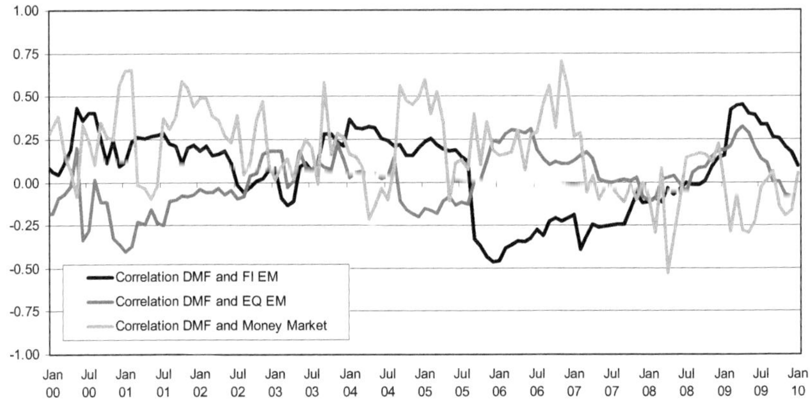

Figure 4-14: 12-months rolling correlations of selected asset classes and DMF[128]

[128] Bloomberg data as of February 2010. Own calculation with indices shown in Figure 6-1.

	MM USD	EQ World	EQ EM	FI World	FI IL	FI EM	FI CRE	FI HY	FI CB	FI CAT	HF	PE	REITS US	COM	FI MF
Money Market USD	1.00000														
Equities World	0.02943	1.00000													
Equities EM	-0.00459	0.86957	1.00000												
Gov Bonds World	-0.09833	0.14582	0.07979	1.00000											
Gov Bonds Inflation Linked	-0.03980	0.42271	0.37568	0.75491	1.00000										
Gov Bonds EM	0.03038	0.61573	0.65827	0.30112	0.51333	1.00000									
Credit Bonds	-0.05590	0.54646	0.53900	0.67049	0.85404	0.70871	1.00000								
High Yield Bonds	-0.06420	0.73183	0.75103	0.14642	0.49095	0.81247	0.75272	1.00000							
Convertible Bonds	0.01661	0.83679	0.80815	0.26958	0.51525	0.68061	0.76728	0.77806	1.00000						
Cat Bonds	0.21415	0.25017	0.25187	0.14822	0.29353	0.32435	0.39924	0.38536	0.38226	1.00000					
Hedge Funds	0.16149	0.61849	0.69243	0.10713	0.37210	0.54131	0.61074	0.62353	0.80773	0.42659	1.00000				
Private Equity	0.14268	0.75028	0.74156	-0.12899	0.14972	0.52125	0.36721	0.64256	0.67055	0.26396	0.63885	1.00000			
Reits US	0.03892	0.77844	0.69470	0.24692	0.52524	0.58985	0.63712	0.72374	0.61374	0.26077	0.44534	0.64073	1.00000		
Commodities	0.09318	0.38279	0.44101	0.12074	0.40811	0.27613	0.40928	0.36396	0.42811	0.24243	0.46720	0.36192	0.35042	1.00000	
Dexia Microfinance Fund	0.34026	-0.02302	-0.07841	0.07578	0.07975	0.04480	0.00594	-0.01078	-0.09172	0.09072	-0.06219	-0.09452	0.05118	-0.17810	1.00000

	MM USD	EQ World	EQ EM	FI World	FI IL	FI EM	FI CRE	FI HY	FI CB	FI CAT	HF	PE	REITS US	COM	FI MF
Money Market USD	1.00000														
Equities World	0.09113	1.00000													
Equities EM	0.11144	0.90752	1.00000												
Gov Bonds World	-0.03486	0.21464	0.19356	1.00000											
Gov Bonds Inflation Linked	0.03224	0.60309	0.58848	0.72586	1.00000										
Gov Bonds EM	0.01924	0.69595	0.72923	0.38605	0.72626	1.00000									
Credit Bonds	-0.02771	0.70114	0.69352	0.61544	0.84895	0.83028	1.00000								
High Yield Bonds	-0.03518	0.81212	0.78643	0.16451	0.61952	0.84971	0.82528	1.00000							
Convertible Bonds	0.06074	0.88081	0.88099	0.30251	0.68238	0.79984	0.86022	0.89385	1.00000						
Cat Bonds	0.22273	0.26365	0.25173	0.21705	0.35241	0.37747	0.47194	0.43120	0.40549	1.00000					
Hedge Funds	0.22106	0.71473	0.80579	0.08772	0.51484	0.57253	0.64197	0.74291	0.81609	0.44706	1.00000				
Private Equity	0.10909	0.78484	0.73199	-0.06876	0.31199	0.55442	0.46240	0.70978	0.62837	0.26612	0.63982	1.00000			
Reits US	0.07878	0.91224	0.79453	0.28209	0.60027	0.73012	0.68836	0.80362	0.78219	0.26751	0.59223	0.79410	1.00000		
Commodities	0.07659	0.53863	0.58305	0.08263	0.52654	0.35868	0.46187	0.49685	0.50212	0.25113	0.62925	0.46761	0.41884	1.00000	
rAGMicrofinance Fund	0.45813	-0.30108	-0.31273	0.03709	-0.11192	-0.23839	-0.18522	-0.30940	-0.29071	0.03528	-0.18393	-0.23394	-0.28018	-0.08859	1.00000

Figure 4-15: Correlation matrix (incl. DMF; 12/1998 – 12/2009)

Figure 4-16: Correlation matrix (incl. rAGMF; 12/2004 – 12/2009)

4.4.2 responsAbility Global Microfinance Fund

The responsAbility Global Microfinance Fund (rAGMF) is a public microfinance debt fund with moderate equity exposure. The fund is managed by responsAbility Social Investment AG and was set up in 2004. Indeed, it is among the most prominent microfinance funds and has a NAV of USD 477 million.

The rAGMF invests mainly in debt instruments issued by MFIs. Furthermore, the fund prospectus allows fair trade and up to 10% equity investments. The fund allocates investments in Africa, Asia, Eastern and Central Europe as well as Latin America. The rAGMF seeks to achieve an annual return above money market.[129]

The main return characteristics of the rAGMF are shown in Figure 4-17. The annualised return of the USD tranche has been 4.11% since inception. The fund made several provisions in 2009; however no defaults happened as yet. In microfinance, the fund is known for conservative valuation for both equity investments as well as debt obligation provisioning. The Sharpe ratio of the fund is 1.35. Again, this high risk-adjusted return key figure is mainly due to the low volatility of microfinance fund performances.

Investment period	12/2004-02/2010
Return	4.11%
Risk	1.24%
Risk free rate (during period)	2.44%
Sharpe Ratio	1.35

Figure 4-17: Key figures responsAbility Global Microfinance Fund

The correlation matrix of the rAGMF reveals low and mainly negative correlations to other asset classes (see Figure 4-16). The USD money market is the only asset category with a significant positive correlation (0.45). The correlation matrix illustrates the attractiveness of microfinance investments from a risk perspective. The

[129] responsAbility (2009), p. 2.

negative correlations to almost all asset classes generate diversification potential. However, correlations may drift in different market situations.[130]

The correlation of the DMF and rAGMF in the last five years was about 0.41. The correlation tends to be high. However, the market distortions during the last two years affected the funds differently. On the one hand these effects are caused by currency hedges. On the other hand a different provisioning policy had an impact on returns. As a result, the correlation was very volatile during the investigated period.

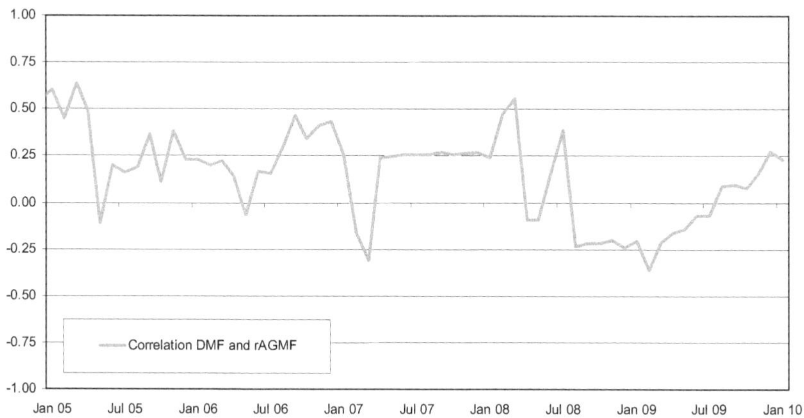

Figure 4-18: 12-months rolling correlation of DMF and rAGMF

4.4.3 Structured products

Structured products such as collateralized debt or loan obligations (CDOs or CLOs) are also marketed. The first microfinance CDO structure was implemented in 2004 – the BlueOrchard Microfinance Securities I (BOMSI) (see Figure 4-19 for an example structure). Structured products are less regulated than funds and are generally closed-end funds with a time horizon of 5-7 years. For this reason, the vehicles

[130] During the financial crises the correlations of many asset classes increased dramatically. From 2008, the diversification potential of several asset classes lowered. One prominent example is the USDEUR exchange rate and its correlation with equity markets. A strong EUR correlates with positive equity markets, whereas in stress situations the old reserve currency USD is favored.

often invest in one period according to the vehicle's maturity. Consequently, diversification considerations are somehow limited and the risk profile of the long-term debt obligations also differs from microfinance investment funds.

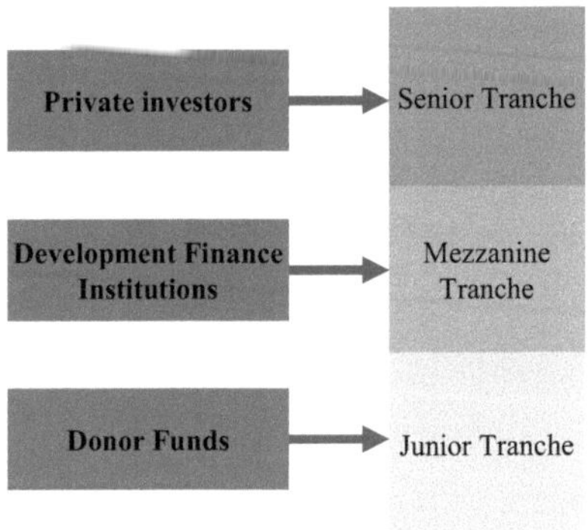

Figure 4-19: Illustrative structure of a microfinance CDO vehicle

In 2005 to 2007 several microfinance CDO or CLO structures were set up.[131] But the current financial crises stopped the success story of this new structure for institutional and private microfinance investments. Besides the closed-end vehicles, the European Fund for Southeast Europe (EFSE) offers an open-end structure. It was set up in 2005 and is the largest microfinance vehicle with close to USD 1 billion assets under management. However, the funds definition of microfinance is questionable, for example it allows loans up to USD 100.000.[132]

4.4.4 ProCredit Holding

The ProCredit Holding is the most prominent microfinance equity opportunity. The German holding company was founded in 1998 and owns 22 banks operating in emerging countries in Eastern Europe, Latin America and Africa. The core business is the provision of banking services to small- and medium-sized entrepreneurs as

[131] CALLAGHAN ET. AL (2007), pp 120.
[132] EFSE (2010), p 1.

well as low and middle income savers. For this reason, focus areas are microcredits and savings deposits.[133]

ProCredit Holding offers equity stakes to investors. Due to their holding structure it is one of the few options to build up a major microfinance equity stake. Unfortunately, ProCredit Holding is not publicly listed. Hence, equity valuations are performed quarterly and access is limited. Accordingly, at the current stage of research a quantitative analysis of microfinance equity stakes is not feasible.

4.5 Microfinance investments in an asset allocation framework

The quantitative analysis of microfinance data contains some major limitations. A derivation of return estimates, risk and correlation expectations would be a prerequisite for an integration of microfinance into an asset allocation framework.

First of all, a clear understanding of microfinance investments is necessary. The MIVs debt obligations with MFIs are booked at par value, besides some very few exceptions with provisions in 2009. This implies a hold to maturity strategy with no default risk. Hence, except from foreign exchange or interest rate hedging no volatility affects contracted debt obligations. In the case of a hard currency, non-interest rate hedging vehicle volatility of returns solely applies from roll-over effects due to interest rate level variations. Accordingly, in many cases the volatility of returns is only affected by a shift in the portfolio of debt obligations.

In finance, several investments with a low volatility of returns due to the investment structure exist. Two prominent examples for this are private equity and real estate funds. In both cases, non-publicly listed open or closed-end funds, the investments are not valued on a daily or even monthly basis. Generally, an expected return over a certain period is modelled and a more or less linear profit shown, provided no unexpected provisions apply. However, for the same asset classes publicly listed vehicles emerged. These publicly listed vehicles with a liquid secondary market reveal a significantly higher volatility of returns than non-listed illiquid

[133] For more information please refer to www.procredit-holding.com.

vehicles.[134] Obviously, the volatility of returns is often used as a risk parameter in asset allocation. Hence, the differences of vehicle structures have to be considered. In conclusion, a distinction of market valued and not market valued asset classes or indices is key in asset allocation.

The volatility of returns gives a risk indication for market valued investment vehicles. Market prices reflect risk factors such as credit or business risks perceived by investors. Therefore the volatility of the prices is an indicator for risks perceived from market participants according to available information. Asset classes or indices representing products without a liquid secondary market have no market prices. Moreover, they do not include risks in prices. Consequently, the volatility of returns has no risk indication in illiquid markets or if no secondary market exists. Investments of MIVs are in an illiquid market and hence the volatility of returns is not an adequate measure for risk.

A quantitative analysis of microfinance investments reveals no meaningful risk and correlation parameters for asset allocation purposes. As outlined above, all calculations based on the volatility of monthly returns are misleading. Hence, the volatility as a risk parameter and correlation figures are inappropriate for asset allocation purposes. A different approach to derive those parameters for microfinance investments needs to be developed. On the one hand, risk parameters of the underlying investments can be consulted. This includes for example figures such as the portfolio at risk of MFIs defined by payments more than 30 days in default (PAR30). On the other hand, a qualitative approach such as scenario analysis can be considered.

A derivation of expected returns for microfinance from past data is meaningless. Firstly, the data history is too short. Indices of MIV investments such as the Symbiotics50 index have about five years of monthly data. Moreover, the oldest single fund with monthly data started in 1998. Therefore, the available data do not include a broad economic spectrum and a full economic long-term cycle. Secondly, the

[134] For example, a non-listed LGT Capital Partners private equity vehicle reveals a volatility of monthly returns of about 9% from 2000-2010, whereas as listed private equity vehicle from the same company has about 27% for the same period. Hence, in this comparison the volatility of monthly returns of a listed vehicle is 3 times higher than the one of a non-listed vehicle.

valuation methodology described above prevents a meaningful attribution of returns to economic cycles. Non-liquid products cushion the perceived risks of investors in crisis situations, because the prices cannot fluctuate according to market perception. Consequently, a backward-looking quantitative analysis of returns is no adequate instrument for future return expectations of microfinance investments.

Overall, a quantitative analysis of microfinance return, risk and correlation parameters is not an adequate methodology for asset allocation purposes. The short history, specific valuation concepts and the absence of a liquid secondary market for microfinance investments require a different approach. Instead of the common quantitative approach, in this case a qualitative methodology might generate more convincing results. The scenario thinking is such a qualitative approach that also fits into the asset allocation concept. The method advises to bring experts from the relevant topics together. Moreover the mixture of asset allocation and microfinance experts implementing a structured evaluation process is one of the most profound qualitative approaches. In conclusion, a scenario process regarding microfinance investments may generate sound return, risk and correlation parameters and hence enable an integration of microfinance into an asset allocation framework.

4.6 Summary

Microfinance is commonly defined as financial services for the poor. A subcategory of microfinance is microcredits, but the distinction in public is inexact. Microcredits are credits for entrepreneurs in the emerging market. Hence, the size is relatively low resulting in high operating costs. Besides individual credits, group and community lending emerged primarily in Asia and Africa to reduce operating costs and minimize defaults. As a result, defaults have been on a moderate level also during the financial crisis. Microcredits are allowed by MFIs, which sometimes already have a banking license and than also can take deposits. One refinancing source of MFIs is the international capital market. However, the market for MFI debt obligations is still small and illiquid. Therefore only some dedicated microfinance funds and investment vehicle participate. However, the market potential is still huge and investments via public funds offer exposure to debt obligations of MFIs or in some cases even equity. Up to now, no debt obligation defaulted even during the financial crisis. In some workout cases the backing of microfinance by supranational or governmental organizations such as IFC or KfW has proven to be supportive. Thus the assessment of microfinance investments in an asset allocation context is complex as no proven track record throughout a whole business cycle exists and emerging asset classes often also have a mission drift.

5 Scenario Process Microfinance

In this chapter the scenario process microfinance is outlined. This process was set up to analyse the methodology in general and the effects of microfinance in asset allocation specifically for this study. The author organised this scenario analysis with experts from scenario analysis, microfinance, asset allocation and emerging markets. The process was generously backed by the Asset Allocation and Research department of LGT Capital Management.

5.1 Setup

5.1.1 Defining the goal

Experts from various fields will elaborate developments for microfinance investments within the next 5-8 years using scenario methodologies. The objectives are a generation of potential scenarios and a determination of return, risk and correlation parameters in the respective states.

Microfinance is an emerging investment topic. A well-balanced asset allocation for investors of any kind may include any potential asset class, because besides return and risk, diversification effects and liquidity are also essential criteria. These parameters cannot be defined adequately with quantitative analysis of historic data for new investment topics or investment categories without a liquid secondary market, both conditions are true of microfinance. Hence, the quantitative tools generally used in finance do not enable the generation of a sophisticated asset allocation. Therefore a qualitative approach using scenario methodologies reveals additional and more adequate information.

In modern portfolio theory, the expected return and risk of an investment are considered as prevailing. Additionally, the current financial crisis demonstrated the importance of liquidity. In general, asset managers take those parameters into consideration to define their asset allocation. Hence, the analysis of risk, return and in the broader sense liquidity is relevant. In detail, normally economic scenarios are developed using growth and inflation as key parameters and expected return, risk and in some cases liquidity in each scenario are modeled by a quantitative analysis of historic data.[135]

The allowance of microcredits to entrepreneurs increased significantly over the last few years. Institutional and private investors are able to participate in this trend with vehicles investing in equity or providing loans to MFIs. During the last years, microfinance became an investment topic with steady excess returns[136], but a certain illiquidity of investments. Thus, microfinance is a potential asset class for balanced portfolios. However, the empirical knowledge of investors is limited, quantitative data are missing and hence a quantitative analysis is misleading.

For this research, a comprehensive scenario process led by scenario specialists of the Daimler Society & Technology Research Group (Daimler STRG)[137] takes place. Asset allocation and investment specialists from LGT Capital Management (LGT CM)[138] as well as microfinance experts met for three workshops to develop and analyse scenarios for microfinance. The objective is the elaboration of expected risk, return, and correlation parameters that enable an integration of microfinance in an asset allocation framework.

5.1.2 Methodology

The future framework conditions and the potential of microfinance investments in emerging markets for the next 5-8 years are investigated with scenario thinking. The evaluation of development paths, potential market size and regional differences are subordinated objectives in the process of modelling microfinance scenarios. Furthermore, a derivation of asset allocation parameters such as return, risk and correlation measures in the acquired scenarios will conclude the scenario process.

The methodology of the scenario process must allow a smart integration of the results into an asset allocation framework. Therefore, the characteristics of asset

135 In general, past periods with similar characteristics are defined and the average value is taken as a proxy for the expected value.

136 Excess returns are returns higher than the corresponding money market returns.

137 The Daimler STRG is a think tank within Daimler Group. Prof. Minx is heading a team of 40 researchers of various fields. The research group has gained experience with several scenario analysis tools for many years. Besides projects across the group the team oversees external projects on a sporadic basis. Furthermore, Prof. Minx teaches at FU Berlin, TU Berlin and FHTW Berlin.

138 LGT Capital Management provides traditional asset management services for LGT Group and external partners.

allocation processes have to be considered. In this process, the asset allocation framework is rather unrestricted due to the optimization of the weighted average of the scenarios. A different approach would be optimising different regimes and in a second step find the optimal asset allocation according to the regime weighting (see Figure 3-10).[139] However, in this case limitations for the scenario matrix would apply as the regimes must be the same for every asset class. As a result, the asset allocation framework chosen allows more variance and asset class specific scenario thinking. Accordingly, a scenario approach with many degrees of freedom is implemented. Consequently, a broad range of descriptors is possible and a 2x2 scenario matrix can be identified with an uncertainty-impact matrix. Moreover, the integration of a wild card scenario is feasible. Finally, an asset class specific scenario framework evolves and a wide discrepancy in the scenario world is created.

A focus of this scenario process is the derivation of quantitative figures from the scenarios. This step is crucial as it is the link between scenario thinking and the asset allocation framework. Firstly, the figures required for the asset allocation framework need to be defined. Secondly, a structured process and thought-out tools have to be developed. Thirdly, according to the developed scenarios an adoption of the tools is required. In this case, group thinking processes and questionnaires are developed to identify expected risk, return and correlation parameters for microfinance investments.

The definition of indicators and signposts is the final step of the process. The implementation of a monitoring process results from these parameters. As a result, the probability of the scenarios can be changed or if necessary new scenarios or even a new scenario process can be set up.

5.1.3 Setup of process

A scenario process requires a detailed structure and procedure. In a first step, a definition of the objective and the applied scenario methodology takes place. Furthermore, the time frame for the process is defined roughly. Subsequently, the participants are advisedly selected. According to objective, methodology, time

[139] For a more detailed insight refer to chapter 3.5.

frame, budget and participants' know-how, a schedule for the scenario process is formulated. A rough schedule of this process is depicted in Figure 5-1.

Figure 5-1: Schedule of scenario process microfinance

The objective and methodology of this scenario process were defined by the author and scenario experts from Daimler AG. Budget and time constraints were agreed on with the financial and most prominent intellectual capacity sponsor LGT Capital Management. The participants represent three different, however sometimes overlapping, backgrounds: asset allocation, microfinance and emerging markets. As a result, the coordination team including Dr. Frank Ruff, Dr. Burkhard Järisch (both Daimler AG) and the author decided on the following structure: firstly, an introduction evening with several presentations on microfinance, secondly, two two-day workshops for the scenario process and thirdly, a one-day finalization day with the key participants. Consequently, this comprehensive structure requires a lot of additional work in between the workshops, but also allows integrating very prominent experts, whose time budget is limited.

An introduction evening for non-microfinance experts was set up as a first meeting. The goal was creating a common know-how basis as most of the emerging markets or asset allocation experts were not familiar with profound microfinance knowledge. Furthermore, a first get-together started the group-building process already before the first workshop.

The scenario process was split in two workshops of two days each. The coordination group arranged a scenario thinking methodology that fitted the strict schedule. As a result, some research and a substantial description process had to be separated from the workshops and were delivered by the author and one participant. However, this also allowed the various experts and senior people to focus on key questions and the displeasure of written formulation of discussed details was kept on a low level.

Finally, a closing day with the key participants was organized to present the results of the process and discuss implementation details. Furthermore, this day also provided the platform for process feedback and discussing further scenario project ideas.

5.1.4 Team selection and participants

The team selection is a crucial procedure for the success of a scenario process. Firstly, experts for the given problem set as well as some people with a broad general education are demanded. Secondly, the emotional intelligence and group thinking are further essential selection criteria. As a result, the author put a lot of time and persuasiveness into selection and winning of participants. Additionally, the participation of some key persons to foster a potential later microfinance investment of LGT CM was considered in the team selection process. However, mentioning that neither participants nor moderators got a financial compensation for their efforts is important. [140] Consequently, the participation was intrinsic and not financially motivated. The only compensation was gaining new experiences, know-how and contacts in the fields of microfinance, asset allocation and scenario analysis.

First of all, the process requires scenario expertise and moderation capacity. A first time solo effort is condemned to fail. Hence, the author decided to consult scenario experts. Daimler AG has a think tank unit (society and technology research group – STRG)[141], which implements scenario thinking for internal and sometimes external projects. In December 2008, a first meeting with the head of the unit Prof. Dr. Eckard Minx[142], Dr. Frank Ruff and Dr. Burkhard Järisch took place. Finally, it was decided that Daimler STRG would moderate the process and take the lead in providing scenario methodologies into this process. Dr. Ruff and Dr. Järisch, two

---

[140] The asset allocation & research department of LGT Capital Management generously financed all costs of the scenario process, which were mainly travelling expenses and seminar costs,

[141] The think tank unit STRG is one of the most prominent think tanks in Germany. About 50 highly qualified and specialised experts from various academic and scientific fields provide research for Daimler AG and also contribute in external research commissions.

[142] Prof. Dr. Eckard Minx is one of the leading innovation experts in Europe. From 1992 to his retirement in 2009 he was the head of the Daimler STRG unit.

experienced scenario process experts, joined the scenario process coordination team with the author.

The next step is the selection of experts in the field of the problem set. In this case, it includes microfinance, asset allocation and emerging markets. Ideally, a scenario process consists of about 12 participants. Accordingly, the objective was to put a team of at least three experts for each field and three generalists together. The key selection criteria for the specialist in each field included expertise, openness for innovative approaches, capacity for team work, social competence and of course availability. The selection process determines the knowledge composition of the process team. Consequently, the team selection provides the basis for the scenario process (see Figure 5-2).

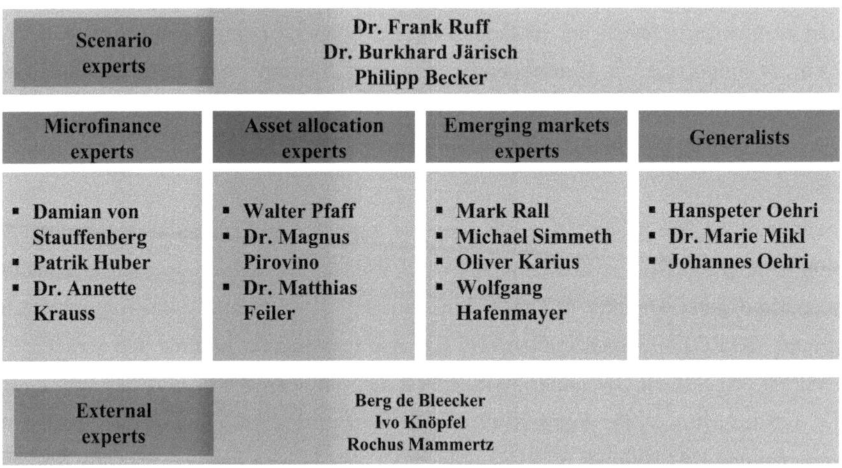

Figure 5-2: Team of scenario process microfinance

Microfinance

Microfinance is a wide subject and, consequently the selected participants have preferably different backgrounds. At a microfinance conference in October 2008 in London, the author got to know Damian von Stauffenberg. Von Stauffenberg founded MicroRate[143], the first rating agency for microfinance institutions in 1997 and has served as its CEO until 2009. MicroRate was designed to provide transparency and in that way attract commercial funding sources to microfinance. Prior to starting MicroRate, von Stauffenberg worked with the World Bank and its private sector affiliate, the International Finance Corporation (IFC) for 25 years. Von Stauffenberg is widely referred to as a pioneer of the microfinance industry and continues to develop new ideas for promoting its growth. His expertise is widely known and in demand, for example in February 2010 he appeared in front of the US Congress to speak about the state of microfinance. In January 2009, von Stauffenberg was convinced to join the process in Switzerland, although he is based in New York.

Other major players in the microfinance industry besides rating agencies include microfinance investment vehicles, development financing institutions, MFIs, microfinance investors and academia. For the process, the perspectives of MIVs, investors and academia were still missing. MFIs were not prioritised as on the one hand, they have a very local perspective and on the other hand, almost all microfinance experts have very detailed know-how about MFIs. The same applies for DFIs, for example Damian has worked over 25 years for the IFC.

As a MIV representative Patrik Huber joined the scenario process. Huber is member of the board of responsAbility social investments AG[144], one of the major microfinance fund providers. He has been with the company since responsAbility's launch and played a key role in developing various investment products, the company's investment processes, and related systems. Prior to this, he worked on various private banking projects at Credit Suisse.

Dr. Annette Krauss completed the microfinance competence. Krauss is the head of the Centre for Microfinance at the University of Zurich. Besides academic research and teaching, the centre seeks a practical focus. Before this, Krauss worked

143 Microrate is one of the two major global rating agencies focusing on microfinance.

144 responsAbility is backed by well-established Swiss financial institutions and a social venture capital company as founders and shareholders. It has a focus on microfinance investments and is one of the major microfinance investment managers.

as a training manager of the United Nations Capital Development Fund and was a senior lecturer of the Kellogg School of Management.

Furthermore, several experts of the microfinance industry were won to give input to the process as external experts. Interviews were organised with Berg de Bleecker, PGGM[145] Investment Manager Responsible Equities Strategies, Ivo Knöpfel, CEO OnValues[146] and Rochus Mammertz, Head of Equity Investment responsAbility Social Investments AG (industry leading regulation expert).

Asset Allocation

The asset allocation expertise in this process was represented by LGT Capital Management staff. Walter Pfaff is Head of Asset Allocation and Research and Dr. Magnus Pirovino former CEO of LGT CM and current Senior Investment Advisor bringing both very senior and thoughtful asset allocation know-how into the process. Furthermore, Dr. Matthias Feiler, a quantitative analyst at LGT CM, contributes with the know-how of latest academic research.

Emerging Markets

Several experts with in-depth emerging market know-how also participated. On the one hand, two fund managers from LGT CM Mark Rall, Head of Investment Management Fixed Income, and Michael Simmeth, Head of Multi Manager Products, both managing emerging market debt funds added their expertise. On the other hand, two start-up, small enterprise and venture specialists with emerging market focus joined the process. Oliver Karius and Wolfgang Hafenmayer both leading the LGT Venture Philantrophy[147] contributed with crucial emerging market small enterprise insights.

Further expertise

Hanspeter Oehri, a senior portfolio manager at LGT CM and advisor to the board added more than 30 years of investment and financial market expertise. In the fi-

[145] PGGM is a Dutch pension fund. It is one of the biggest institutional microfinance investors globally.
[146] OnValues is an investment advisor based in Zurich. Besides mainstream investments, OnValues focuses on investment solutions including social returns.
[147] LGT Venture Philanthropy provides solutions for philantrophic engagement. The objective is to raise the quality of life sustainably for the less advantaged people in developing countries.

nance industry his well-performing funds are known for the behavioural finance investment concept.

Dr. Marie Mikl and Johannes Oehri completed the team. Mikl has a background in biology and broadened the teams' horizon. She is a project manager for LGT&Science, an initiative that fosters collaborations with universities. Oehri added fresh ideas and talent capacity as he finished his University of St.Gallen diploma in 2008. He is currently working as a Financial Economist for LGT CM.

5.2 The process

The scenario process passed through seven steps as outlined above. Each step was taken during the workshops with the participants.

5.2.1 Preparations

5.2.1.1 Field of study

The problem set of the scenario analysis was determined by the scenario and coordination team. In various discussions, the scenario experts and the author defined the topic addressing the problem set in a way adapted to scenario analysis. The scenario process answers the problem set of "*Future framework conditions and potential of microfinance in emerging and developing market 2015+*". This includes a time horizon, a broad regional definition and a structured analysis of the issue.

The problem set was also introduced to all participants of the scenario analysis. Firstly, in the invitation for the process and secondly, it was outlined and discussed at the beginning of workshop I. This discussion appeared relevant to get a common understanding of the issue. In this case, the regional definition was challenged, but finally agreed on in consensus.

5.2.1.2 Introduction evening

The first group meeting was a microfinance introduction evening. The meeting took place on May 25, 2009 in LGT facilities in Pfäffikon/SZ. The group's know-how regarding microfinance was very diverse. Besides the microfinance and some emerging markets experts, the knowledge of microfinance was rather basic. Therefore, Dr. Annette Krauss and the author gave two presentations of one hour each followed by an intensive interactive discussion. The first presentation focused on the financial side of microfinance giving an overview, introducing the market players and microfinance investment vehicles as well as discussing current risks for microfinance investments. This was followed by a talk "Opening the black box: how microfinance institutions work" focussing on the direct impact of microfinance for MFIs and clients. As a result, the evening gave a detailed insight into microfinance and the participants got to know each other. Thus, in the following weeks the participants followed microfinance market news closely via newsletters[148]. Furthermore, a get-together after presentations and a one hour question and answer session promoted further discussions on microfinance as well as it enabled a first group-forming process.

5.2.2 Workshop I

The first scenario analysis microfinance workshop took place in Schloss Freudenfels, Switzerland on June 4-5, 2009. Schloss Freudenfels is a small convention centre for up to 25 persons in a secluded area close to Stein am Rhein. Thus, it allows focusing on a specific topic and supports team building as distraction is rare.

The workshops started with team building and process introduction. The team building and integration of scenario and microfinance experts who could not join the introduction evening was a key element. Furthermore, the coordination team introduced the scenario methodology and the problem set, both of which were discussed intensively. Consequently, a generally accepted basis was set and agreed on by all participants.

5.2.2.1 Impact factors

Following the determination of the problem, the participants divided into groups of four to brainstorm impact factors for "*Future framework conditions and potential of microfinance in emerging and developing market 2015+*". In a plenary session, the gathered impact factors were presented and similar factors were revised. However, in this step it is not a must to withdraw highly correlated or unimportant parameters. The uncertainty-impact matrix will anyhow reveal those issues. Anyway, elimina-

---

148 All major microfinance players offer weekly or monthly newsletters.

tions at this stage of the process economise the capacities. Finally, 29 factors resulted from this brainstorming session (Figure 5-3).

No	Descriptor	No	Descriptor
1	Liberalisation of capital markets	16	Securitisation of credit risks
2	Protectionism	17	Quality of due diligence on single credits
3	Volatility of EM FX	18	Development of microcredit market
4	Regulation of financial service providers	19	Development aid policy - consideration of MF
5	Measurability of social return of microcredits	20	Perception of MF investment track record
6	Reputation of microcredits in EM	21	Intensity of competition in MIV market
7	Cultural acceptance of financial services in EM	22	Commercial interest of MIV investors
8	Professionalism of MFIs	23	Systemic leverage in microfinance
9	Demand of microcredits in EM	24	Governmental incentives for investors
10	EM growth	25	Transparency of MIVs (and their investments)
11	EM inflation	26	Generation of a secondary market for MF
12	Market structure in MFI segment	27	Volume of international capital in EM
13	Risk-adjusted return of microcredit investment	28	Know-how of financial markets about MF
14	Hedging instruments for not credit specific risk	29	EM capital flows
15	Governmental regulation of MFIs		

Figure 5-3: Descriptors in scenario process microfinance

5.2.2.2 Factor projections

Thereafter, the descriptors were discussed and projections for these factors resolved. In three subgroups, the participants focused in detailed discussion on selected descriptors. At least one expert for microfinance, asset allocation and emerging market joined each subgroup. The factors were described in more detail, including the current state and indicators for changes. Moreover, these working groups outlined potential future states of the factors. The path and reasoning of these factor projections were described, but also concise titles resolved (see Figure 5-4). As a result, a detailed description of all 29 descriptors including definition, indicators, status quo and up to three projections was developed.[149]

[149] An exemplary factor description is shown in Appendix– 1.

No	Descriptor	Projection A	Projection B	Projection C
1	Liberalisation of capital markets	ongoing	changeless	delibaralisation
2	Protectionism	increasing	changeless	decreasing
3	Volatility of EM FX	increasing	changeless	decreasing
4	Regulation of financial service providers	increasing	changeless	decreasing
5	Measurability of social return of microcredits	measurable	hardly measurable	
6	Reputation of microcredits in EM	improving	changeless	deteriorating
7	Cultural acceptance of financial services in EM	increasing	changeless	decreasing
8	Professionalism of MFIs	increasing	changeless	decreasing
9	Demand of microcredits in EM	strongly increasing	moderately increasing	changeless
10	EM growth	high	normal	low
11	EM inflation	high	normal	low
12	Market structure in MFI segment	strong consolidation	moderate consolidation	fragmentation
13	Risk-adjusted return of microcredit investment	outperformance	normal	underperformance
14	Hedging instruments for not credit specific risk	existing	not existing	
15	Governmental regulation of MFIs	increasing	changeless	decreasing
16	Securitisation of credit risks	excessively	moderately	not existent
17	Quality of due diligence on single credits	improving	changeless	deteriorating
18	Development of microcredit market	strongly	moderately	changeless
19	Development aid policy - consideration of MF	increasing	changeless	decreasing
20	Perception of MF investment track record	improving	changeless	deteriorating
21	Intensity of competition in MIV market	increasing	changeless	decreasing
22	Commercial interest of MIV investors	increasing	changeless	decreasing
23	Systemic leverage in microfinance	strongly increasing	moderately increasing	changeless
24	Governmental incentives for investors	increasing	changeless	decreasing
25	Transparency of MIVs (and their investments)	strongly improving	moderately improving	changeless
26	Generation of a secondary market for MF	existing and liquid	existing and illiquid	not existing
27	Volume of international capital in EM	strongly increasing	moderately increasing	changeless
28	Know-how of financial markets about MF	increasing	changeless	
29	EM capital flows	strongly increasing	moderately increasing	decreasing

Figure 5-4: Factor projections of descriptors

5.2.2.3 Classification of descriptors

An uncertainty-impact matrix was used as a tool for step four of this scenario analysis. The descriptors were evaluated regarding their impact on microfinance framework conditions and their probability. First of all, the participants discussed this task in groups of four and finally every single participant evaluated the impact and the probability of those 29 descriptors. However, every participant had 29 points for impact and 29 points for probability. These all had to be used evaluating the 29 descriptors by assigning 0, 1 or 2 points to each descriptor. Thereafter, the points were summed up and an uncertainty-impact-matrix applied (see Figure 5-5).

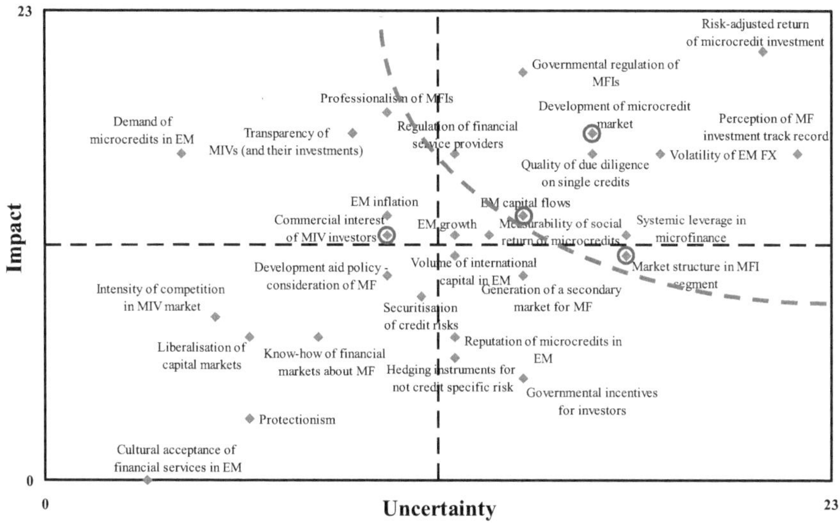

Figure 5-5: Uncertainty-impact matrix

In matrix 5-4, the top right hand corner is particularly important. In the area marked by the dotted line the descriptors have a relatively high impact and a high uncertainty regarding the scenario question. Hence, these descriptors are favourable to span a scenario cross. On the one hand, they open up a broad range of outcomes (projections). On the other hand, they also have a high impact. Two of these descriptors span a scenario cross with four possible scenarios. For example, if the projection of a descriptor is very uncertain, the projections are nearly equally weighted or at least any scenario field has a certain probability. If it is furthermore an important factor with high impact, it is a key driving force of the problem set. Consequently, two uncertain and important factors are preferred for the scenario matrix. The selection of these factors is outlined in the next section.

5.2.2.4 Scenarios

The scenario matrix exhibits the basic scenario features and is defined by two descriptors. In step five, the selection of descriptors from the uncertainty-impact matrix to span the scenario cross takes place. In this case, a 2x2 scenario matrix was applied to keep the amount of scenarios limited (see Figure 5-6). Preferably, these two factors are from the top right hand corner of the uncertainty-impact matrix. However, the combination of those two must also be reasonable. Usually, the scenario matrix shall be conducted by more general factors. At best, impact and uncertainty are somewhat uniformly distributed. Moreover, a macroeconomic factor may help the participants to build a solid base, whereas a specific microfinance factor may give the typical framework.

In an intense discussion, participants outlined that various "uncertain-impact" factors are not eligible for a scenario matrix. Several factors appeared to be very specific in the microfinance segment or financial markets. This includes factors such as "quality of due diligence", "volatility of EM FX", "systemic leverage", "risk-adjusted return of microfinance investments" and "perception of track record". Of course, these factors can have a huge impact and are uncertain. However, most of them have an impact especially in negative cases such as "quality of due diligence", "volatility of EM FX" and "systemic leverage". In conclusion, some of these factors are more important for wild card scenarios than a scenario matrix. Moreover, the descriptor "risk-adjusted return of microfinance investments" and "perception of track record" are close to the goal of this scenario analysis. As a result, they should not be included in the scenario cross.

A scenario matrix was decided with "EM capital flows" and "development of microfinance market" as axes. Taking the previous discussion into account, the participants chose a macroeconomic and a microfinance specific factor. "EM capital flows" measure the flow of money in or out of the EM. "Development of microfinance" market describes the infrastructure provision and development of microfinance regarding regions and products. Both descriptors are in the uncertain-impact spectrum of the uncertainty-impact matrix. Accordingly, these two factors span a scenario matrix with four scenario fields. Next, the participants split into groups of three[150] to enrich the scenarios with projections of the other 27 remaining descriptors. Finally, this process created well-defined scenarios and suitable scenario titles were chosen (see Figure 5-6).

[150] Again, all subgroup teamwork processes had the intention of broad group expertise. Therefore all groups consisted of an expert for microfinance, asset allocation and emerging markets.

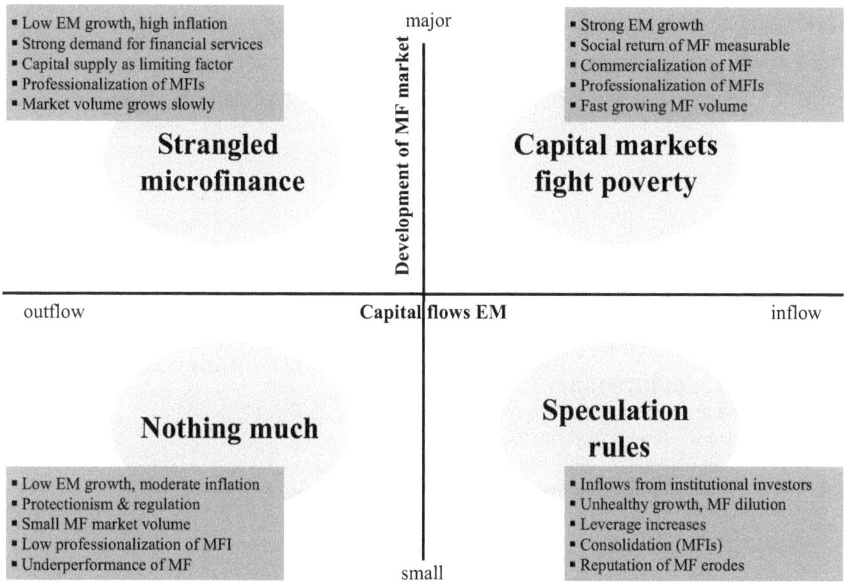

Figure 5-6: Scenario matrix "EM capital flows" and "development of MF market"

Furthermore, a second scenario matrix was selected. This enhances the variety of possible scenarios and increases incidents. Moreover, a wild card scenario was introduced to generate a "black swan" scenario (see Figure 5-7). For the second scenario matrix, the participants decided to choose two different factors. The above discussed exclusion of several factors with high impact and high uncertainty for the scenario matrix limited the number of potential scenario matrix factors. As a result, the participants decided to allow in one exceptional case also the inclusion of a factor even though it is not in the top right hand corner. As a result the last available factor of the top right hand corner "market structure in MFI segment" was chosen. Furthermore, the factor "commercial interest of MIV investors" was selected as axes in the second scenario matrix, because the microfinance market is currently at the turning point of pure social investors to also financial motivated investors. However, a scenario including a fragmented market structure and decreasing commercial interest of investors seemed very unlikely. Hence, it was decided to analyse a wild card scenario instead of a scenario with decreasing commercial interest and a more fragmented market structure. Again, the participants split into groups of three[151] to enrich the three remaining scenarios and formulate the wild card scenario.

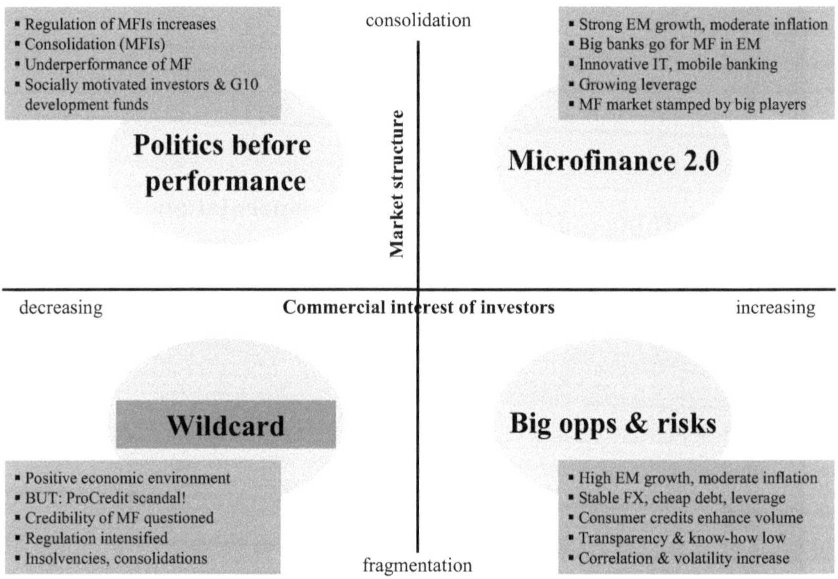

Figure 5-7: Scenario matrix “market structure” and “commercial interest”

The scenario process generated seven conclusive scenarios and one wild card scenario. However, the participants and scenario teams decided to reduce the number of scenarios for the further process for two reasons. Firstly, the focus allows a concentration of the capacities. Secondly, a selection can also reduce the overlap or similarity of scenarios. This aspect is essential in a scenario process and can be illustrated with the scenario funnel.

[151] See footnote 150.

A comparative analysis of the scenarios unveiled the overlaps of scenarios. On the basis of this analysis, the goal was to reduce complexity and proceed with four scenarios and the wild card scenario. The participants stated that the scenario "microfinance 2.0" widely overlapped with the scenario "capital markets fight poverty". It was decided to proceed with the latter scenario as it seemed more realistic. Furthermore, the participants agreed that a further fragmentation of the microfinance market structure was nearly impossible and hence the scenario "big opportunities & big risk" was excluded. Thirdly, the participants indicated that capital outflows from the emerging markets are very unlikely, especially if microfinance markets develop. Thus it should only be considered in one scenario. Hence, the scenario "strangled microfinance" was not considered in the further process. In conclusion, the participants decided to focus on the scenarios "capital market fight poverty", "nothing much", "speculation rules" and "politics before performance". Finally, these scenarios were scripted and enriched with further details in between workshop I and workshop II. The following paragraphs provide a brief overview of these scenarios written from a backward-looking perspective in 2015.

Scenario description "capital markets fight poverty"

The macroeconomic conditions reveal a clear leadership of emerging markets after the financial crisis. The emerging markets took advantage of an ongoing liberalization trend, increased their influence in international committees and strengthened domestic markets. Thus, the prospering economies increased intra-EM trade and had growth rates of more than 7%. Furthermore, inflation rates remained on a moderate level of 6-11%. As a result, strong capital inflows into the emerging markets resulted and came along with slightly appreciating currencies.

In the years 2009-2015, microfinance has become a mature asset class. Investors considered a merely low correlated asset class with interesting fixed income return potential. Furthermore, the social return of microfinance attracted investors and in 2012 several companies offered a social return analyzer. Consequently, commercialization of microfinance investment increased. Furthermore, MIVs adapted a low leverage of about 10% instead of cash levels they had in previous years to meet investors' return expectations. As a result, the number of MIVs increased and also a liquid secondary market for MFI debt obligation transactions emerged.

In the aftermath of the financial crisis, the authorities increasingly tightened the regulatory framework for MIVs and MFIs. However, the transparency for investors was not significantly increased. Nevertheless this was not a main concern for investors that wanted to participate in the booming market. Thus, first critics arose. For instance Thorsten Hens, Prof. for Behavioral Finance at the University of Zurich stated in the Neue Zürcher Zeitung (NZZ) in June 2013: "This investor's behavior can be disastrous as we might know especially since the securitization of mortgage-backed securities some years ago".

The competition in the microfinance business increased slightly, because inflows increased dramatically and sufficient funding for MFIs was in the market. Thus, also demand for microcredits grew tremendously and multiplied over the past six years. As of today (2015), the market serves 300 million clients and it has a volume of more than USD 250 billion. The funding of MFIs changed in this environment. Nowadays, more than 50% (in 2009 about 20%) of the volume is financed by foreign credits. Moreover, synergy effects led to some consolidations, which did not attract attention due to the strong market growth. Furthermore the MFIs enhanced the product segment and distribution channels to extend customer retention ("cross-selling"), but also to attract new clients. As a result, MFIs generated synergies and reduced operating costs. Thus, the return on equity increased sharply and made stakes in MFIs attractive.

In line with balance sheet growth, MFIs hired more employees. During the last years, the recruiting and training of employees was a core task for MFIs. However, many MFIs were trapped in the strong market growth and organization, while processes and structures of MFIs suffered. As a result, in various MFIs the credit quality is very questionable and it seems as if many consumer credits were in the credit portfolios. Thus, one might expect higher default rates. This and the huge impact on the regional economy have caught the attention of authorities and in some countries nationalizations have taken place last year.

Scenario description "nothing much"

The macroeconomic conditions in the emerging markets became gloomy. A short and sharp recovery after the financial crisis was only a short term effect. Later on, the developed countries stabilized but the emerging markets became very heterogeneous. Countries exporting to developed countries and also having an increasing domestic demand such as Brazil and China continued to grow, whereas several countries in Central and South America (e.g. Ecuador, Nicaragua, Venezuela) as well as Africa (e.g. Nigeria, Ghana) suffered severe depressions. Overall, the growth rate for emerging markets in the last five years was below 2% with China and Brazil being exceptions. However, at least the inflationary pressure was moderate with 6-11%. Furthermore, protectionism became an increasingly used instrument of international politics in accordance with increasing intervention of regulatory authorities in trade business. As a result, most countries noted capital outflows and depreciating currencies.

The worsening macroeconomic situation made debt obligations for MFIs unattractive. On the one hand, currency depreciation increased the pressure on MFIs with unhedged debt obligations and caused some defaults. On the other hand, the funding of microcredits had to become more local. The foreign funding shrunk from about 20% in 2009 to only 10% in 2015. As a result, the MFIs had to generate more deposits and also reduced the credit volume. Therefore, MFIs focused on their core business and did not extend the product segment widely. The increased funding costs and the remaining high operating costs did not allow profitable business models. Furthermore, the main challenges such as management quality, training of employees and risk management were not tackled. As a result, due diligence of micro-entrepreneurs was weak and default rates increased slightly. Thus, authorities increased their regulations but could not act efficiently. In most cases the bureaucracy for MIVs and MFIs increased with no major impact on risk management or control.

The reputation of microfinance shrunk and investors reallocated their money. However, the first years have been promising. In 2009 and 2010 investment in MIVs more than doubled. But return expectations were not met and the underperformance for example to emerging market sovereign debt did not convince financially motivated investors. Thus, socially motivated investors and the sovereign or quasi sovereign investors remained the pillar of microfinance. Some G10 countries decided to increase microfinance investments as a new form of development aid. In this market environment many service segments of the microfinance industry declined. International rating agencies for instance reduced their effort in microfinance from 2012 onwards. The remaining three specialized rating agencies divided the market and have no major incentives anymore. As a result, the transparency for investors did not increase at all.

Scenario description "speculation rules"

The recovery of the world economy from the financial crisis was mainly driven by emerging markets. After a sharp rebound in the years 2009 and 2010, growth rates of emerging markets decreased in the following years. However, economic growth of about 5% with a moderate inflation of slightly above 6% was still far better than in developed countries. As a result, the emerging markets profited from capital inflows and thus the currency appreciated slightly.

The capital was also attracted by microfinance. Major institutional investors entered the market seeking attractive returns and a sustainable investment. However, the microfinance industry was not able to allocate the money accordingly. As a result, money flowed into countries and segments that could deal with the huge inflows. Thus, mature MFIs acting in urban areas attracted the money. Consequently, the social status of microfinance eroded and microcredits were increasingly consumer credits. Furthermore, MFIs were not fostered to enhance their product segment or increase their regional focus. At this stage, the MFIs driven by profit maximization increased the leverage and the credit lending policy loosened further. Neither credit assessments were improved nor were creditors in default suited. As a consequence, the default rates increased steadily and the balance sheet of MFIs was only backed by ongoing inflows. In this situation, a consolidation phase started. Major players took over smaller competitors mainly to increase their balance sheet and significance. Thus, the microfinance market more and more had a risk concentration.

MIVs benefited from major inflows. Their business model finally became very profitable, but the increased allocation of money was in line with lowering standards of due diligence. MIVs were just not able to deal with the increasing asset under management. Furthermore, in such an environment more transparency for investors was not required. In fact, MIVs put more effort in creating a secondary market to enhance the liquidity of their portfolios and have a market valuation for the debt obligations. Socially motivated investors became more and more dissatisfied and finally in 2014 some of them made a statement against the "misbehavior of financial markets in a social environment" and withdrew their money. However, the microfinance industry was not affected anymore by this minor investor group and the business went on. In 2015, the market reached a volume of about USD 200 billion outstanding credits funded primarily by international capital markets.

Scenario description "politics before performance"

The macroeconomic conditions do not have a major impact in this scenario. However, the financial crisis caused a shift in regulatory policies globally which had a major impact on microfinance. The increased operating costs of MFIs due to regulatory issues triggered a wave of consolidations. Major market players took advantage of the opportunity to increase their regional scale and acquired smaller niche MFIs. Synergy effects kicked-in only partially and several integrations failed due to the centralized management.

From an investors' point of view, MIVs performed not as expected compared to other asset classes. Thus, financially motivated investors were not attracted or even exited the microfinance market. However, investors with a social motivation remained invested and even generated moderate inflows. A main reason for this was the introduction of a new methodology to measure social returns in 2011. This enabled investors to market their social investment accordingly. Moreover, governmental and supranational investors became able to prove the social responsibility of their microfinance investments. As a result, these institutions increased their exposure in microfinance. In addition, the development aid policy was more and more shifted to microfinance.

The shift of the investor structure decreased the competition among MIVs. Furthermore, MIVs focused increasingly on social returns. Consequently, the interest rate for debt obligations decreased. Moreover, the MIVs efforts for a secondary market resulted in the launch of such a platform in 2012. However, the liquidity is up to now very low. In general, MFIs still source only 25% of their funding from foreign investors. The main funding with finally about 75% are local deposits. The lowered refinancing costs were transferred into better credit conditions, but also used for investments in employee training, risk management and an extended product and regional range. As a consequence, microfinance increasingly gained acceptance and reputation in the emerging markets. The population acknowledges the positive effects of microfinance and thus the payment morale increased steadily. In 2015, the PAR30 is below 1% and merely no write-offs have to be made.

5.2.2.5 Wild card scenario and incidents

In the sixth step of this scenario process the participants developed a wild card scenario. This wild card scenario practically goes hand in hand with the other scenarios. However, it is one of the clues of a scenario analysis to elaborate one or more wild card scenarios. This wild card scenario is triggered by an exogenous shock. This shock can have positive or negative effects on the problem set of the scenario analysis. Hence, first of all the subgroup creating the wild card scenario provided an open list of potential shocks to microfinance (see Figure 5-8). In this case, the participants decided to introduce the "microfinance Madoff" into the scenario process. Besides, the elaborated list of potential shocks for microfinance can be used for an ongoing risk assessment.

Event Risk	Impact
Global illiquidity	Market growth slowing – less allocation of loans, nonperforming loans become visible
Press: "exploiting the poor – rates >50%!"	Transparency and active communication may cushion – short term impact
Bad reputation – negative social impact studies	Social investors de-invest, focus on commercial investors possible
War – e.g. Armenia, Azerbaijan, Georgia	Major impact despite regional diversification
International banks entering the market	Strong competition
Human right on credits for 12%	Easy credits per law, very unlikely
MF organized cooperatively	Limitation of capital and growth
EM hyperinflation	Adaptation to inflation possible (due to short duration), but hyperinflation needs a different approach
Microfinance Madoff	Impact depends on market size

Figure 5-8: Potential exogenous shocks to microfinance

Wild card scenario description "microfinance Madoff"

The recovery of the world economy from the financial crisis was mainly driven by emerging markets. After a sharp rebound in the years 2009 and 2010, growth rates maintained at a high level, whereas the developed countries were not able to find the path to sustained growth. The growth rates in the emerging markets were close to 10% with a moderate inflation of about 6%. Thus, the very attractive macroeconomic conditions attracted huge capital inflows resulting in moderately appreciating currencies.

The microfinance industry managed to take advantage of the good conditions and the volume increased steadily. Both social and financial return pleased the investors. Furthermore, MIVs were able to increase the quality of the due diligence. Accordingly also MFIs increased their standards for credit assessments, risk management and employee training. The reputation of jobs in microfinance increased tremendously and MFIs were able to attract educated people. As a result, MFIs' management became very professional and the product as well as regional range was extended. Microfinance investors also increased their know-how of the industry. On the one hand, major institutional investors gained experience. On the other hand, microfinance investment consultants became an industry standard. As a result, until 2013 the transparency of the market as well as the know-how and competence of all involved parties increased.

However, in April 2013 a major shock hit the microfinance industry. A major conglomerate of 50 MFIs with a consolidated balance sheet of USD 20 billion went bankrupt due to mismanagement and accounting fraud. The microfinance investors were worried and many withdrew their capital immediately. MIVs did not have sufficient liquidity and most of them had to close their funds causing a shock wave among investors. Even more dramatic scenes became obvious in the emerging markets. The clients with deposits at MFIs panicked and started to withdraw their money. As a result, also many MFIs got into liquidity problems resulting in some countries in a bank run. Finally, the authorities in emerging markets reacted and decided that major MFIs had to take over the smaller ones. However, nowadays in 2015 the market still suffers as international capital markets lost confidence in microfinance investments. At least the reputation within the emerging markets was through the interventions of the government partially restored.

5.2.3 Workshop II

The second scenario analysis microfinance workshop took also place in Schloss Freudenfels, Switzerland on July 9-10, 2009.

5.2.3.1 Derivation of implications

The derivation of implications is the key process of any scenario analysis. This holds particularly true in this case, because return estimates and risk parameters of microfinance as well as correlations with other asset classes are the objective of this scenario process.

In the second workshop, the participants discussed implications of the developed scenarios. At first, the participants split in groups of three[152] and debated on the impact as well as chances and risks of each scenario for the main players – debtors, MFIs, MIVs and investors. Thereof, implications for current positioning and actions were discussed. Subsequently, those results were compared between all scenarios including the wild card. In conclusion, the participants became acquainted with the scenarios after the four-week break between the workshops.

The derivation of return estimates played an essential role in the second workshop. Hence, the scenario implications for investors were analysed in two steps. Firstly, the qualitative implications in the microfinance market were assessed (referring to Figure 4-2). For example, in the scenario "nothing much" hedged interest rates for debt obligations are expected to decrease slightly due to higher FX hedging costs. Moreover, the default rate strongly increases. This is caused by a stagnating microfinance market and low economic growth resulting in a bad portfolio quality of MFIs. Microcredits default increasingly and often macroeconomic conditions force debtors to use credits partially for comestibles. Microcredits are extended with increased frequency leading to over-matured portfolios. Furthermore, MIVs have higher expenses for regulation, lobbying, marketing and of course tightened due diligence. This leads to higher operating costs of MIVs.

In a second step, the participants derived return estimates for microfinance equity and debt investments (referring to data of Figure 4-10). In the next paragraph a detailed description for the assumptions of microfinance debt returns is outlined.

In June 2009 investors of MIVs had an annualised return of about 6%. In the scenario "capital markets fight poverty", the interest rate for debt obligations between MIVs and MFIs remain at about 9%. Moreover, the defaults of these are

[152] See footnote 150.

expected to increase very slightly to 1%. Furthermore, MIVs are able to reduce their costs to about 1.5%. As a result, in the scenario "capital markets fight poverty" the participants expected a slight increase of returns to 6.5%. In the scenario "nothing much", several factors deteriorate. Firstly, the interest payments of debt obligations are with roughly 8% about 1% lower due to higher FX hedging costs. Secondly, the default rate increases from 1% to about 4%. And finally, the total expense ratio increases by 1% to 3%. As a result, the participants estimated that the expected return in the scenario "nothing much" is about 1% instead of 6%. In the scenario "speculation rules" the interest rate for debt obligation lowers due to the competitive market to about 7.5%. However, due to the huge money inflows MIVs are able to cut their costs by 50% and charge only slightly more than 1% fees. As a result, in the scenario "speculation rules" the participants estimated the return to be about 5.5%. In the scenario "politics before performance" the participants expect a lower interest rate for debt obligation to MFIs. Driven by social motivated investors the interest lowers to 7%. The ongoing consolidation increases defaults to about 2%. The fees of MIVs are unchanged. As a result, in the scenario "politics before performance" the participants estimated an annual return of about 3%. This structured approach was also conducted in all scenarios for equity returns (see Figure 5-9).

	Capital markets fight poverty	Nothing much	Speculation rules	Politics before performance
Return expectation MF debt	6.5%	1%	5.5%	3%
Reasoning	Rates remain, slight increase of defaults, slight cost reduction	Rates decrease moderately, strong increase of defaults, operating cost increase	Rates decrease, defaults increase slightly, operating costs decrease	Rates decrease, defaults increase, operating costs remain
Return expectation MF equity	30%	-30% (either ~0% or ~-60%)	45%	24% (either ~48% or ~0%)
Reasoning	Increasing leverage, 10x market growth	MFIs diverge: increasing defaults & costs (regulation), leverage remains, depending on extent	High leverage, multiples increase from 2x to 4x book, 5x market growth	MFIs diverge: Regulation increases operating costs, some MFIs can generate scale effects to cushion

Figure 5-9: Return expectations for MF debt and equity in described scenarios

The derivation of a risk parameter for the scenarios is complicated. As mentioned in chapter 4.5, the analysis of volatility parameters is inappropriate. Thus, an analysis of the risks in the underlying structure might be a proxy. Hence, PAR30 and write-offs of MFIs might give an indication. These parameters were analyzed in the quantitative derivation of returns for the estimated defaults costs of MIVs. As a result, the expected defaults of debt obligations are a proxy for some components of risk in microfinance debt investments.

	Capital markets fight poverty	Nothing much	Speculation rules	Politics before performance
Provisions for defaults of debt obligations	0.5-1%	4%	1%	2%

Figure 5-10: Expected risk proxied by expected defaults of debt obligation

Additionally the risk-adjusted attractiveness of microfinance might be a proxy for risks. This measure was chosen, because individuals cannot define "risk" adequately. Nevertheless, the participants were able to rank the risk-adjusted attractiveness of asset classes in each scenario. For this reason, the participants completed a questionnaire evaluating 10 asset classes including MF debt and equity in the four scenarios and the wild card scenario (see Appendix– 2). The analysis reveals that microfinance debt investments are attractive on a relative basis only in two of the five scenarios. In the remaining scenarios and the wild card, microfinance debt investments are expected to be relative unattractive on a risk-adjusted basis. Microfinance equity investments seem to be more attractive from a participant's perspective (see Figure 5-11).

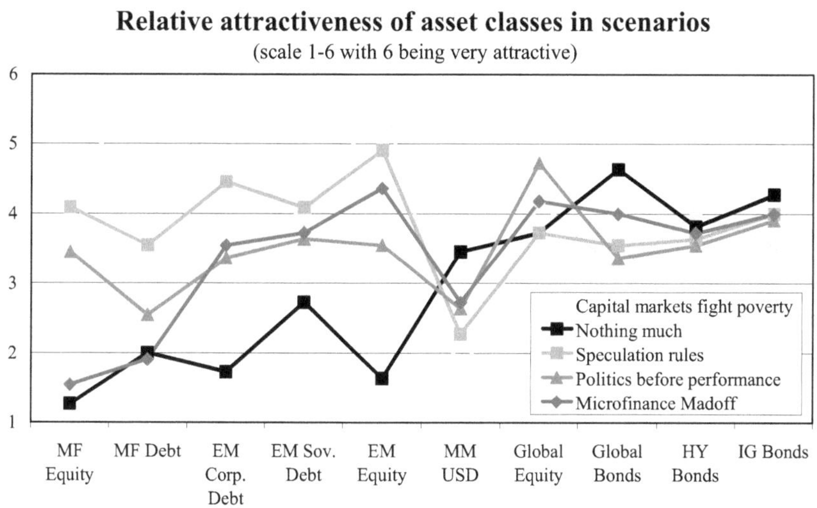

Figure 5-11: Relative attractiveness of asset classes in each scenario

The weighted average of all scenarios reveals the relative unattractiveness of microfinance (see Figure 5-12). The participants consider the risk-adjusted return of microfinance debt investments as underperformer. A money market investment is the only asset class that is expected to be less attractive. However, the risk-adjusted return does not include a diversification effect which has to be considered for asset allocation. In conclusion, microfinance offers valuable returns, but the participants estimated the risk-adjusted attractiveness as underperforming compared with other asset classes.

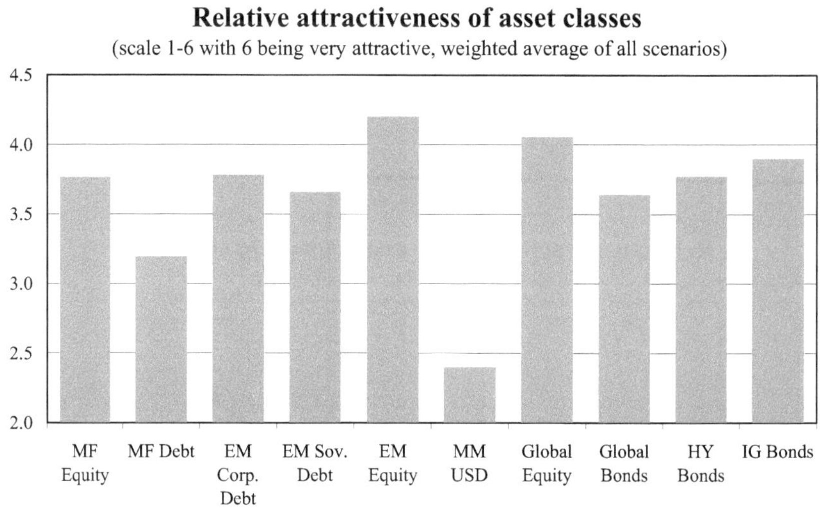

Figure 5-12: Relative attractiveness of asset classes overall

The derivation of correlation parameters is a complex intention. Up to now, many microfinance experts merchandise the story of microfinance as being uncorrelated to other asset classes. As market data are rare, in this study the correlation was derived by a questionnaire (see Appendix– 3). The participants were asked to evaluate the correlation of five asset classes (EM sovereign bonds, EM corporate bonds, EM equities, MF debt and MF equity) with 11 macroeconomic and market factors such as growth, inflation, public debt and commodity prices. Accordingly, the cross-correlation of microfinance and these asset classes via macroeconomic factors indicates a proxy for correlation.[153] The evaluation of the questionnaire unveils a clear correlation of microfinance along with other asset classes. Indeed, it seems obvious that economic growth or high commodity and food prices affect all asset categories including microfinance. However, the correlations are not extensively high (see Figure 5-13). As a result, this study clearly rejects the assumption of microfinance being an uncorrelated asset class.

	EM corp. debt and MF debt	**EM sov. debt and MF debt**	**EM equity and MF debt**
Correlation	~0.7	~0.6	~0.4

	EM corp. debt and MF equity	**EM sov. debt and MF equity**	**EM equity and MF equity**
Correlation	~0.5	~0.4	~0.6

Figure 5-13: Correlation of microfinance with other EM asset classes

The final step in the process of deriving implications was the assessment of the probability of occurrence. Consequently, participants analysed the probability of occurrence of each scenario and as well the divergence of each scenario from the status quo (see Figure 5-14). This analysis contributes to various calculations such as weighted overall parameters. Furthermore, the measure variance from status quo

[153] In detail, the estimated correlation coefficients of all participants are summed for one factor. In a next step, a quotient of the summed estimated correlations with increasing EM growths of microfinance debt and for instance EM equities is calculated. The same is performed for all 11 factors. The quotient has to be in the interval from -1 to 1. Finally, the mean of the 11 quotients generates a correlation estimate for the two asset classes, in this example for microfinance debt and EM equity.

illustrates the impulse for change and hence creates awareness for change. Additionally, the participants estimated the coverage of these scenarios. On average, the participants expect that the four scenarios and the wild card come close to about 80% of future states. In conclusion, the process generated four nearly equally weighted scenarios that are assumed to cover about 80% potential futures.

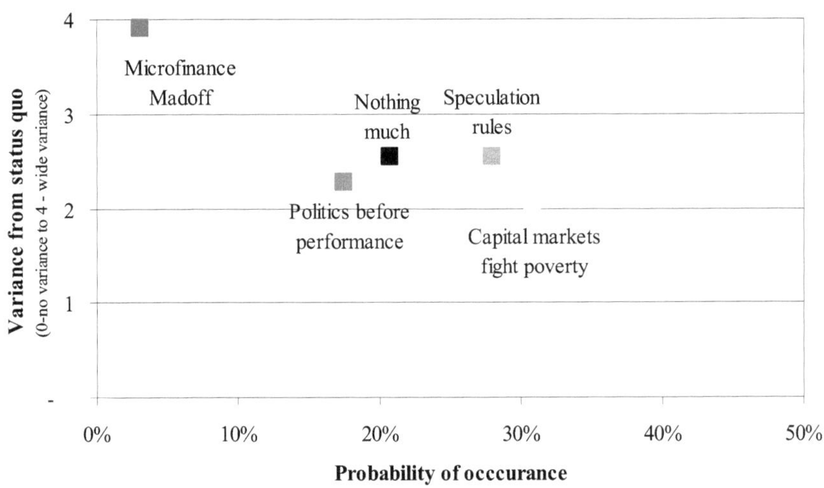

Figure 5-14: Probability of occurrence of described scenarios

5.2.4 Closing day

A third workshop took place in Pfäffikon SZ on July 17, 2009. The main objective of this meeting was a review and résumé of the scenario process microfinance. Furthermore, the final step of the scenario process was discussed. However, the scenario team had decided during the planning phase to hold this workshop only with key members of LGT Capital Management and the scenario team of Daimler AG.

5.2.4.1 Indicators and signposts

The definition of leading indicators and signposts enables an identification of the scenario path. These indicators are generally descriptors of the scenario process, because they allow an assignment of the real world to the developed scenarios. Thus, parameters such as the leverage of MFIs, the market structure or the PAR30 were defined and integrated into a monitoring cockpit indicating the scenario path. In addition, sources for these indicators were analyzed. For example, the formation of a governmental incentive system such as tax remissions on returns for microfinance investors can be monitored in the press or regulation specialists and lobbyists might provide the information even in advance. As a consequence, a comprehensive monitoring cockpit evolves.

Indicator	Sources for indicator
Leverage of MFIs	Rating agencies, MIVs
FX-volatility	Bloomberg, own model
(Governmental) incentive system for investors	News, regulation specialists
Measurability of social return	Academic studies, SAM, GTZ
Professionalization	Expert questionnaire (local agents)
Market development: mobile banking	Expert questionnaire (local agents)
Market development: urban vs. rural	Expert questionnaire (local agents); volume, profitability
Due Diligence: consumer lending	Data of rating agencies
Volume of demand	TheMix, MicroRate, CGAP
Market structure	MFIs/volume
Investment indicator of MIVs	MIVs' investment model
PAR30 and write-offs	MIVs, MFIs, rating agencies

Figure 5-15: Indicators for a monitoring cockpit

5.2.4.2 Scenario process feedback

The participants of the scenario workshop provided their feedback at the end of workshop II. In workshop III, the scenario team discussed this feedback and analyzed the whole scenario process with key members of LGT Capital Management.

First of all, the group dynamic was discussed. The participants mentioned that the motivation curve was varying significantly. At the beginning, the team was excited. However, on the second day of workshop I the uncertainty-impact valuation of descriptors was the emotional bottom. The process as well as some descriptors seemed unclear. Nevertheless, the scenario team tried to motivate the participants with the next conceptual step and a break. The development of scenarios in subgroups was the turning point in the process. The participants reaped the rewards of their hard and partially vague exercises beforehand. As a result, during the later process all participants formed a close group during the process work and in the evenings as well.

The scenario experts Dr. Ruff and Dr. Järisch explicitly highlighted the excellent selection of participants. On the one hand, the subgroups' expertise was well-balanced with experts of all fields needed and broad know-how. On the other hand, the solidarity and strong company of participants during the workshop and beyond was said to be exceptional for scenario processes. In conclusion, the selection of participants turned out to be a success.

The results of the process were analyzed critically. Firstly, the selection of descriptors and the development of scenarios were evaluated very positive by participants and the scenario teams. Thus, the basis of scenario analysis was commonly accepted. Secondly, the derivation of quantitative results was discussed more critically. On the one hand, the very positive equity return expectations were challenged. It might be the case that a group spirit influenced the process resulting in very high or very low estimates. On the other hand, it was explicitly said that the correlation would be expected to be dynamic and not static. However, this is a general problem in asset allocation processes and not specific for microfinance. Consequently, the scenario experts from Daimler AG perceived the process to be very profound, well thought through and at any time critically challenged by the participants.

The participants enjoyed scenario thinking and the innovative atmosphere of being out of business in the remote conference venue Schloss Freudenfels. It was clearly stated that this promoted "out of the box thinking" and of course increased the focus of participants on the workshop. Exceptionally, the participants succeeded in taking phone conferences, portfolio decisions, as well as executive board meetings in well in advance defined workshop breaks. As a result, very productive and focused workshop sessions, as few as possible daily business calls and pleasant leisure periods formed a unique and long-lasting experience.

LGT CM executives were impressed by the scenario tool as well as microfinance as an asset class. Several participants became convinced of scenario thinking as a powerful tool for various problem sets. Specific methods of the process are already being used in several processes. Furthermore, various problem sets are in pipeline for further scenario processes. In addition, in the meantime LGT CM has introduced microfinance debt investments in a balanced and a bond fund of a sustainable product family. Moreover, a reunion of the Freudenfels microfinance scenario participants took place on January 21, 2010 in Zurich. Finally, the amicable relations and established close ties across various backgrounds are a major benefit of this scenario process for all participants.

5.3 Implications of scenario process microfinance for asset allocation

The scenario process microfinance allowed an estimate of asset allocation parameters. During the process, return, risk and correlation parameters were derived from scenarios. These scenarios were built on a five to seven year time horizon. Hence, they match the time frame of a strategic asset allocation. In conclusion, the outlined scenarios generate adequate parameters of microfinance debt and equity investments for an asset allocation framework.

5.3.1 Parameters for the asset allocation framework

Return estimate

The return estimates for microfinance debt and equity are directly modelled during the scenario process (see Figure 5-16). On average, for microfinance debt investment, a return of 4% is expected. The overall return for microfinance equity investments is estimated to be about 20%. These two return estimates can be introduced directly into an asset allocation framework.

	Capital markets fight poverty	Nothing much	Speculation rules	Politics before performance	Microfinance Madoff	Overall regime
Weight	31%	21%	28%	17%	3%	100%
Return expectation MF debt	6.5%	1%	5.5%	3%	4%	4%
Return expectation MF equity	30%	-30%	45%	24%	20%	20%

Figure 5-16: Return estimates for microfinance debt and equity

Risk estimate

The derivation of risk estimates from a scenario process is more complex. The parameter "risk" is not obviously visible and measurable for people. However, the process clearly showed the risk components for microfinance investors. These are mainly default risks of microdebtors, foreign exchange risks, operational risks and illiquidity risks. The process allows two different concepts for an estimate derivation. Firstly, the returns for microfinance and the return and risk characteristics of other asset classes allow a derivation of microfinance risk out of the relative attractiveness assessment. Secondly, the underlying risk components are estimated individually and finally they are summed up. However, both approaches measure the same risks. Consequently, one would expect similar risk estimates.

The risk derivation from the relative attractiveness assessment of asset classes by workshop participants reveals a significant risk of microfinance. The participants scored microfinance debt to have one of the most unattractive risk/return profiles (see Figure 5-12).[154] Hence, in a ranking of asset class risk/return profiles, microfinance debt should be also among the least attractive asset classes. Global and EM government bonds have the worst return/risk profile according to return and risk parameter of asset classes outlined in chapter 6 and hence microfinance debt should have an even worse one. As a result, this method indicates that the process participants expect for microfinance debt a return/risk quotient of less than 0.4. A quotient of 0.4 would correspond to a risk of 10%. For microfinance equity investments, a quotient of about 0.45 applies (see Figure 5-17). As a consequence, the return esti-

[154] An analysis with Sharpe ratios instead of risk/return figures reveals very similar results.

mates of the scenario process and these return/risk quotients indicate a risk for microfinance debt of about 12-15% and microfinance equity of about 40%.

	Expected return	Expected risk	Return/risk	Rank	Rank process
Equities World	8.5%	18.0%	0.47	2	2
Equities EM	11.5%	25.7%	0.45	3	4
Gov Bonds World	3.0%	7.0%	0.43	5	6
Gov Bonds EM	4.0%	11.0%	0.36	6	7
Credit Bonds	4.5%	9.1%	0.49	1	1
High Yield Bonds	5.5%	12.7%	0.43	4	5
Microfinance debt	4.0%	*13.3%*	*0.30*		8
Microfinance equity	18.0%	*40%*	*0.45*		3

Figure 5-17: Rank of risk/return analysis and participants' assessment[155]

A second approach applies by adding the risk components. This analysis is outlined for microfinance debt only. An in-depth analysis of microfinance equity risk was not performed in the scenario analysis process.

The first risk component is the default risk driven by the underlying business model. This risk is highly correlated with the default risk of the underlying microcredits. Overall, participants estimated a default risk of about 1.75% (Figure 5-18).

	Capital markets fight poverty	Nothing much	Speculation rules	Politics before performance	Microfinance Madoff	Overall regime
Weight	31%	21%	28%	17%	3%	100%
Default risk	0.5-1%	4%	1%	2%	2%	1.75%

Figure 5-18: Default risk of microfinance debt investments

A second risk component is the foreign exchange risk of the investment. The scenarios are enriched with a projection of foreign exchange volatility, which is highly correlated with hedging costs. Hence, on a hedged basis, the foreign exchange risk

[155] The italic return/risk figures are derived according to the ranking of asset classes. Out of these, a risk estimate is derived according to the return estimate generate in the scenario process.

is implied in the costs for hedging. On average, the scenario process estimates hedging costs of about 2%.

The operational and political risk is a third component of microfinance investment risks. Experts argued during the process that in microfinance operational and political risks are a major risk component directly affecting investments. This includes for example fraud, inappropriate risk management or political interventions. De facto, the result is a default or at least some loss. In contrast to the first risk component, this measure is not driven by microcredits. The operational and political risk is estimated to be about 2%.

The final component for the risk assessment is the illiquidity of investments. The debt obligations have a fixed maturity and are not tradable. Hence, for investors liquidity is limited. According to the illiquidity premium assessment in chapter 6, an illiquidity risk of about 7.5% applies for microfinance debt. As a result, an overall risk figure of about 13.25% results for microfinance debt by adding up the individual risk components of this asset class.

In conclusion, the risk of microfinance debt is estimated to be somewhere in the range of 12-15%. The bottom-up and the top-down risk assessments provide very similar results for microfinance debt investments. For equity investments, the top-down approach results in a risk estimate of about 40%.[156] These risk figures are introduced into the asset allocation framework.

Correlation estimate

The correlation is the third asset allocation parameter. Obviously, for the estimation of forward-looking correlations one needs a clear understanding of several asset classes in every scenario. The complexity of this step is immense. Hence, the above outlined approach was very time consuming. Furthermore, a reduction of the complexity was given by estimating correlations for only three other asset classes. As a result, participants were able to provide an idea for the correlation of microfinance investments with other asset classes (see Figure 5-13). The estimated correlations of

[156] Due to time restrictions a bottom-up approach was not performed during the scenario process.

microfinance investments with emerging market asset classes are used in the portfolio optimization.

5.3.2 Costs of a scenario process

A scenario process is a costly tool. The organisation and inclusion of various experts generates expenses and the process is also very time-consuming. The analysis of one asset class as outlined above includes more than 90 working days of senior and executives working days as well as about 50 days of preparation and process work in addition.[157] Assuming a conservative USD 2'000 per senior day and USD 500 per preparation day, the costs for human capital are more than USD 200'000. Furthermore, five seminar days for 16 people, a kick-off meeting, process planning meetings with the scenario experts as well as travelling expenses have to be taken into account. Consequently, a scenario analysis is a very expensive tool for asset allocation purposes.[158]

5.4 Summary

The scenario process reveals four different futures and a negative impact scenario for microfinance. The scenario set includes very positive as well as negative scenarios for microfinance clients and the microfinance sector. However, in every scenario investors generate positive returns with microfinance debt investments ranging from expected 1%-6.5% per year with a scenario weighted average of 4%. Microfinance equity investments are similar to private equity and thus have a higher volatility with returns ranging from -30% up to 45%. The risk assessment for microfinance debt reveals four risk components. The default risk of the debt obligation, foreign exchange risks in the whole value chain, operational and political risk and finally also liquidity risks of microfinance investments. Overall, microfinance hard currency debt investments have a risk component of about 12-15%. Furthermore the workshop participants expressed a correlation of microfinance investments that is

[157] This includes five workshop days for 14 people (70 days), a kick-off meeting and further study time for two comprehensive pre-read packages (14 days) as well as scenario experts planning time (6 days). Furthermore, the preparation of pre-read packages, wrap-up of materials between the workshops and finalization of the workshop materials adds another 50 working days.

[158] Fortunately, this scenario analysis was sponsored by the Asset Allocation & Research department of LGT CM and by all participants and experts, who did not charge any fees.

clearly above market expectations. The story of microfinance being an uncorrelated asset class is clearly rejected.

6 Asset Allocation Model

In this chapter, an asset allocation model is derived. Firstly, an optimization including several asset classes is performed. Secondly, microfinance debt is introduced into the asset allocation framework with input parameters derived from a quantitative analysis of the past. Thirdly, the qualitative assessment of the scenario process microfinance provides forward-looking return, risk and correlation estimates for the asset allocation framework. Finally, the results are compared and microfinance investment advices for different investor types proposed.

6.1 Data and assumptions

In the following, the data set for the asset allocation optimization is introduced. Return estimates are derived for all asset classes, however, risk parameters are obtained by a quantitative analysis of the past. Hence, besides the selection of asset classes and the underlying parameters, the indices for the derivation of risk parameters are presented.

6.1.1 Selection of asset classes and data

In general, the intention of an asset allocation process is a broadly diversified portfolio allowing an optimal return/risk profile and also taking liquidity aspects into account.[159] Therefore, an integration of a wide set of asset classes in the optimization process increases the diversification potential. As a result, equities, bonds, alternative investments and real assets are considered (see Figure 6-1).

[159] SPREMANN (2008), pp. 2.

Asset Class	Index*
Money Market USD	3-months US Treasury bills (secondary market)
Equities World	MSCI World
Equities EM	MSCI EM
Gov Bonds World	Citigroup Global Bond G7
Gov Bonds EM	JPM EMBI+
Gov Bonds Inflation Linked	Barclays Global Inflation Linked Bond
Credit Bonds	Barclays Global Credit Bond
High Yield Bonds	Barclays Global High Yield
Convertible Bonds	UBS Convertible Bond
Cat Bonds	Swiss Re Cat Bond Index
Hedge Funds	CSFB/Tremont Hedge Fund Index
Private Equity	LPX Major Market
Real estate (REITs)	GPR 250 global
Commodities	Goldman Sachs Commodity Index
Microfinance debt	Dexia Microcredit Fund or scenario data

* All indices are total return and USD hedged

Figure 6-1: Asset classes and respective indices

Money market data are given by 3-months US treasury bills secondary market transactions. This investment is only subject to a US government default within the next three months.

The equity indices are total return indices from MSCI. The MSCI World index is a global equity index of 23 developed markets. The MSCI EM index consists of 23 emerging markets. Hence, there is no intersection of country exposure. In both indices dividends are reinvested.[160] The government bond indices are the Citigroup Global Bond G7 index for developed government bonds[161], the JPM EMBI+ as a standard index for emerging markets government bonds[162] and the Barclays Global

[160] MSCI BARRA (2010).

[161] CITIGROUP (2010). The index consists of G7 government bonds with a par amount of USD 12.620 billion. As of March 2010, the average coupon is 2.91%, the average maturity about 8 years and the duration is 6.3 years. The quality of the index is AA+ and the current spread to Libor -7 basis points.

[162] J.P.MORGAN (2010). The index consists of government bonds from 15 emerging markets with a par amount of USD 201 billion. As of March 2010, the maturity is about 13 years and the duration 7.35 years. The quality of the index is BB+ and the spread to US government bonds 300 basis points.

Inflation Linked Bond index for inflation linked government bonds.[163] Furthermore, the high yield and investment grade corporate bond indices are both Barclays total return indices.[164] The index considered for convertible bonds is the UBS Global Convertible Bond index.[165] Consequently, all these indices are retrieved from Datastream as total return indices and USD hedged.[166]

In the emergent cat bond market, the data history is limited. Swiss Re introduced in January 2002 several cat bond indices based on daily Swiss Re pricing indications.[167] This total return index for all outstanding USD denominated cat bonds is adequate for asset allocation purposes.

The asset classes "hedge funds", "private equity", "real estate" and "commodities" are measured by common listed benchmarks. For hedge funds, the CS/Tremont Hedge Fund index is considered.[168] It includes every hedge fund sector and provides an asset weighted total return performance of the hedge fund industry. The LPX major market index is selected as an index for private equity investments.[169] A listed private equity index is chosen as the illiquid structure of a non-listed private equity vehicle would require a profound understanding of risk and correlation estimates for this asset class. Hence, a further scenario process would be necessary. Therefore, the most common listed private equity total return index is chosen. Real estate investments somehow generate a similar problem. Accordingly, a very liquid investment structure of real estate is selected. The GPR 250 global is an index for real estate investments trusts (REITs).[170] The commodity sector is

[163] BARCLAYS CAPITAL (2010). The index consists of inflation linked government bonds from the US, United Kingdom, France, Japan, Germany, Canada and Sweden with a market value of USD 1.393 billion. The average maturity is about 11.5 years and the duration about 9.5 years.

[164] BARCLAYS CAPITAL (2010). The global credit index consists of corporate bonds with an outstanding market value of USD 8.608 billion. The average maturity is about 7.6 years and the duration 5.25 years. The global high yield bond index consists of corporate bonds with an outstanding market value of USD 1.177 billion. The average maturity is about 7.26 years and the duration 5.4 years.

[165] UBS (2008). The index represents global convertible bonds with an investment grade rating. It is calculated as a total return index.

[166] The corporate and high yield bond indices are total return since inception indices. This methodology is often applied by Barclays (formerly known as Lehman) credit bond indices. As a result, returns can only be calculated by adding 100 to the index measure.

[167] For more detailed information see Swiss Re (2007).

[168] For further information see Credit Suisse First Boston (2010).

[169] For further information refer to LPX (2009).

[170] For further information refer to GPR (2009).

indicated by the S&P Goldman Sachs Commodity index, which is mainly driven by energy components.[171] In conclusion, investments in alternative asset classes, real estate and commodities are proxied by common indices. However, these indices are often criticised to not reflect the respective asset class adequately.[172]

Microfinance investments are focused on microfinance debt. Firstly, fund data from the Dexia Microfinance Fund are considered. This approach is chosen to obtain results according to a standard quantitative asset allocation methodology. Secondly, the forward-looking data generated during the scenario analysis process for this asset class are integrated into an asset allocation framework.

6.1.2 Input parameters for portfolio optimization

The estimation of consistent input parameters is a key component for portfolio optimization processes. The data history of asset classes may give some information about estimated returns, risks and correlations. However, the generation of forward-looking estimates from past data is questionable (see chapter 2.4). It would negate any innovation and change of driving forces. As a result, a qualitative forward-looking estimation of input parameters is a more consistent approach.

A portfolio optimization is mainly driven by return estimates. According to Chopra and Ziemba (1993), the sensitivity of a mean-variance optimization to return estimates is about ten times higher than to standard deviation estimates and about twenty times higher than to correlation estimates. Consequently, correlation estimates and covariance have a minor impact on portfolio optimization.

6.1.2.1 Return estimates

The return estimates are generated by an analysis of a coherent set of regimes developed and implemented by LGT CM. For each asset class the return is estimated in eight macroeconomic regimes with a five year time horizon. These regimes include a "classic boom" scenario as well as a "deflationary depression" scenario. The expected return in every regime is derived by a quantitative assessment of past periods as well as a qualitative assessment of the future. This coherent mixture of both approaches results in a return estimate. Finally, a weighting of the regime

---

[171] For further information see Standard and Poor's (2009).
[172] For the hedge fund universe see for example LHABITANT (2004), pp 87.

applies and hence an overall return estimate for each asset class can be calculated. In conclusion, the return estimates introduced in this asset allocation model are derived from the proprietary LGT CM long-term expected return regime framework.[173]

The return estimate for microfinance debt is generated differently. On the one hand the estimate is based on a quantitative analysis of the Dexia Microcredit Fund. On the other hand the qualitative results of the scenario process microfinance are introduced. All expected annualised returns are shown in Figure 6-2.

Asset Class	Expected return*
Money Market USD	2.0%
Equities World	8.5%
Equities EM	11.5%
Gov Bonds World	3.0%
Gov Bonds Inflation Linked	3.5%
Gov Bonds EM	4.0%
Credit Bonds	4.5%
High Yield Bonds	5.5%
Convertible Bonds	7.0%
Cat Bonds	4.0%
Hedge Funds	5.5%
Private Equity (listed)	12.0%
Real estate (REITs)	8.5%
Commodities	6.5%
Microfinance debt	DMF 4.5% / Scenario 4%

* annualised returns for five year forecast period

Figure 6-2: Expected returns for all asset classes

6.1.2.2 Risk and correlation parameters

The risk and correlation parameters are determined in a covariance matrix. The matrix is modelled with logarithmic monthly returns.[174] A ten year analysis period

[173] The LGT Capital Management return estimates are slightly modified and for proprietary reasons rounded to half percentages.

[174] Money market USD is calculated with 3-months US Treasury bills (secondary market).

is set from January 1999 until December 2009. This also corresponds with the availability of data for the Dexia Microfinance Fund. Consequently, a broad spectrum of market scenarios is included.

The risk parameter is mainly determined by historic standard deviations. However, this backward-looking approach may not include all risk components. A more sophisticated approach would be to implement a forward-looking risk matrix. In this study, the risk matrix is not the main objective. Therefore, the illiquidity risk, the main additional risk not projected in past standard deviations, is added as a risk measure. In conclusion, a standard deviation analysis for all asset classes is conducted on the above mentioned ten year data set and an additional illiquidity risk is added.

Illiquidity is also defined and measured as a risk. Investors have a preference for liquid investment strategies[175] and therefore an illiquidity discount for some asset classes is integrated into the variances and hence also the covariance matrix. In this study, the illiquidity discount of an investment is indicated by its bid-ask spread. However, this spread varies extremely over time. Consequently, the illiquidity is extremely costly in crisis situations, almost exactly when most investors would need liquid markets. Thus, an analysis of bid-ask spreads of all considered asset classes was performed with Bloomberg data or over-the counter offers in October 2008.[176] The equity asset classes (equity developed, emerging and REITs) as well as commodity trades had no major transaction cost disturbance. However, for several fixed income asset classes bid-ask spread increased.[177] Furthermore, also for other asset classes such as hedge funds, private equity and cat bonds the bid-ask spread increased or they were not tradable at all. Microfinance investments for instance were only limited tradable. The debt obligations are not tradable and hence only interest payments and maturing debt obligations generate liquidity. However, in a sell-off the liquidity may not be sufficient to serve redemptions. In conclusion, for several

---

175 SPREMANN (2008), pp. 2. Moreover, SCHOLES & WILLIAMS (1977) triggered research regarding the impact of an assets' liquidity on its parameters.

176 Over-the counter offers are derived from notes of portfolio managers from LGT Capital Management.

177 In some cases, brokers even rejected trades at all, because they did not want to take the risk on the banks balance sheet.

asset classes an illiquidity risk is defined according to the increase of the bid-ask spread in October 2008 (see Figure 6-3).

Asset Class	Illiquidity risk
Money Market USD	0.0%
Equities World	0.0%
Equities EM	0.0%
Gov Bonds World	0.0%
Gov Bonds EM	0.5%
Gov Bonds Inflation Linked	0.5%
Credit Bonds	1.5%
High Yield Bonds	1.5%
Convertible Bonds	1.5%
Cat Bonds	7.5%
Hedge Funds	7.5%
Private Equity (listed)	7.5%
Real estate (REITs)	0.0%
Commodities	0.0%
Microfinance debt	7.5%

Figure 6-3: Illiquidity risk for each asset class

In this asset allocation model process, three different covariance matrices apply. Firstly, a correlation and a covariance matrix excluding microfinance are calculated (see Appendix– 4). Secondly, the initial covariance matrix is complemented by data of a quantitative analysis for microfinance debt investments (see Appendix– 5). These two covariance matrices can be calculated with quantitative analysis of past data supplemented with the illiquidity risk measure.[178] Thirdly, the initial covariance matrix is complemented with qualitative parameter for microfinance debt from the scenario process. The risk of microfinance debt investments is estimated and hence the variance can be calculated. Furthermore, the correlations with emerging equities and government bonds allow the calculation of covariances with these two asset classes. The derivation of correlations with all other asset classes is performed

[178] The correlation of asset classes and the standard deviation define the covariance of two asset classes. All parameters are obtained from the ten year data set with one exception – for the CAT bond index a shorter period applies. Moreover, the illiquidity risk is added to the past standard deviations.

in a factor loading approach following Fama-French (1993). In this study, factor loadings are calculated for each asset class using the correlation of each asset class with the two factors EM equities and EM bonds. As a result, a new covariance matrix with $B'\Omega B$, where B is a matrix of factor loadings and Ω is the covariance matrix of the factors, can be calculated. From this covariance matrix a correlation matrix is derived. In this case, the estimation with just two factors leads to an over-estimation of correlations of all asset classes with microfinance debt. For this reason, just the ranking of the correlations is considered and new correlation estimates are generated in line with the two given correlation estimates for EM equities and EM bonds (see Figure 6-4). Finally, the existing covariance matrix is complemented with the new estimates for microfinance debt (see Appendix– 6).[179] In conclusion, three different correlation and covariance matrices are used in the portfolio optimization process.

[179] The qualitative generation of correlation estimates in a group process is time-consuming. Above all, the qualitative estimation of correlations for several asset classes with market and macroeconomic factors is a complex analysis. Moreover, correlations may vary over time, which was impressively demonstrated during a peak of the financial crisis in fall and winter 2008/09. Therefore, the chosen approach during the scenario process to derive only two correlation estimates for very common asset classes is arguable, but adequate especially with respect to the minor impact of covariance parameters on the portfolio optimization process (see chapter 6.1.2).

	Correlation in factor loading model	Correlation rank in factor loading model	Correlation estimate applied
Gov Bonds EM			**0.5**
Gov Bonds Inflation Linked	0.994	1	0.4
Equities EM			**0.3**
Credit Bonds	0.991	2	0.3
Cat Bonds	0.980	3	0.2
Gov Bonds World	0.976	4	0.2
Money Market USD	0.970	5	0.2
High Yield Bonds	0.888	6	0.2
REITs	0.782	7	0.1
Convertible Bonds	0.773	8	0.1
Hedge Funds	0.675	9	0.1
Equities World	0.535	10	0.1
Private Equity	0.529	11	0.1
Commodities	0.328	12	0

Figure 6-4: Deriving correlation estimates for microfinance debt from a factor loading model

Finally, a parameter set with all required inputs for an asset allocation optimized is defined. Figure 6-5 shows the return estimates and risk assumptions of each asset class as well as a correlation estimate with microfinance based on the quantitative approach and the scenario process.

	Expected return	Expected risk	Expected correlation with microfinance	
			Quantitative approach	Qualitative approach
Money Market USD	2.0%	0.5%	0.02	0.2
Equities World	8.5%	18.0%	0.00	0.1
Equities EM	11.5%	25.7%	-0.01	0.3
Gov Bonds World	3.0%	7.0%	0.00	0.2
Gov Bonds Inflation Linked	3.5%	8.7%	0.01	0.4
Gov Bonds EM	4.0%	11.0%	0.00	0.5
Credit Bonds	3.5%	9.1%	0.01	0.3
High Yield Bonds	6.0%	12.9%	0.00	0.2
Convertible Bonds	7.0%	14.6%	-0.01	0.1
Cat Bonds	4.0%	12.3%	0.00	0.2
Hedge Funds	5.5%	14.1%	0.00	0.1
Private Equity (listed)	12.0%	36.2%	-0.01	0.1
Real estate (REITs)	8.5%	22.4%	0.01	0.1
Commodities	6.5%	26.6%	-0.02	0.0
Microfinance debt	Quant. 4.5% / Qual. 4%	Quant. 8.5% / Qual. 13.5%	1.00	1.0

Figure 6-5: Return, risk and correlation parameters at a glance

6.2 Asset allocation optimization excluding microfinance

In this section, the asset allocation optimization with given parameters excluding microfinance is outlined. For this process, the same model and parameters as in section 6.3 will be used. Accordingly, a direct comparison of the effects of microfinance investments will be possible.

The portfolio optimization process is a mean-variance approach. Several risk profiles of investors are investigated. The idea of this optimization is to set-up a long-term asset allocation. Hence, the transaction costs are excluded and no prior portfolio weights of the asset classes exist. The only constrain is an upper boundary for money market investments of 20%.[180] In Figure 6-6 the optimized portfolios excluding microfinance investments for several lambdas[181] are revealed. Furthermore a Telser shortfall for the optimized portfolio is calculated. The minimum return is set as 0% and the shortfall has a maximum probability 5%.[182]

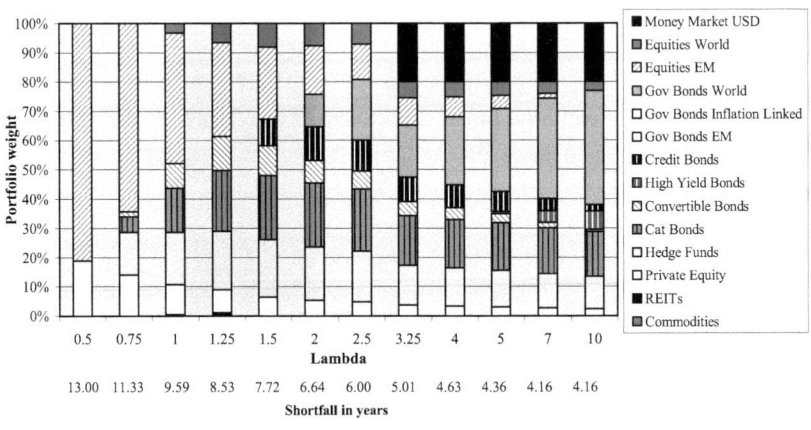

Figure 6-6: Optimized portfolio weights excluding microfinance

[180] Clients are not willing to pay for portfolios that invest strategically considerable amounts in money markets. The maximum money market allocations of funds in practice are about 20-30%.

[181] Lambda is a risk aversion factor of the investor (see also chapter 2.3).

[182] The shortfall concept allows a minimum investment return. In many cases, investors request a positive return. As a result, the minimum return should be 0%. Moreover, a shortfall might occur with a given probability. In this study a shortfall of 5% is chosen.

The optimized portfolios indicate the huge difference between investors. Very risk-averse investors clearly prefer money market, government and special bond investments. As the willingness to take risks increases, investors prefer more risky investments such as convertible bonds or high yield, hedge funds and equity investments. However, in this optimization a clear preference for bond risks over equity risk compared to standard optimization applies. Furthermore, dependent on the investors' risk preference the equity risk is increasingly taken in emerging markets. Finally, this optimization advises risky investors to allocate their wealth mainly in emerging market equities and to some extent in private equity. Four asset classes are not considered in this optimization. Emerging market government bonds and inflation linked bonds have a comparably high risk. However, in a qualitative analysis this result might differ. Moreover, the analysis of commodities and real estate exposure via REITs reveals the high risk of those investments. Therefore, all four asset classes are not considered in any portfolio. In conclusion, the optimized portfolios have a clear preference for credit and bond risks and avoid very high risk asset classes. Credit asset classes such as investment grade, convertible and cat bonds are a major segment as well as hedge funds. This view has also been expressed lately from some experienced investors, e.g. Ray Dalio from Bridgewater.

6.3 Asset allocation optimization including microfinance

6.3.1 Optimization with quantitative microfinance parameters

In this section, the asset allocation optimization with quantitative microfinance parameters introduced in section 4.4 and described in chapter 6.1 is presented.

The portfolio optimization process is identically to the one outlined above for investments excluding microfinance. The only constraint for portfolio weights is a maximum of 20% of money market investments. Figure 6-7 shows the portfolios optimized with quantitatively derived input parameters for microfinance debt investments.

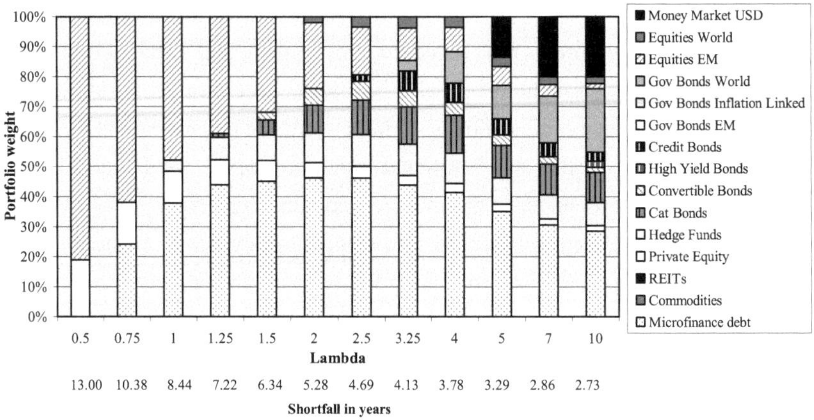

Figure 6-7: Optimized portfolios weights including microfinance (quantitative approach)

Microfinance debt investments have a surprisingly high quota in almost all portfolios. In defensive portfolios a microfinance weight of more than 25% applies. Moreover, with increasing risk more and more microfinance exposure is added at cost of money market and government bond quotas. The exceptions are portfolios with a shortfall markedly above ten years. In these portfolios the allocation focuses on EM equities and private equity. Overall, the portfolios are characterized by the microfinance debt investment. As a result, the high microfinance allocation lowers portfolio risk and hence shortfall markedly.

At first sight the results given by that asset allocation optimization are astonishing. However, the assumptions for microfinance debt investments might not be correct despite adding illiquidity risk. The quantitative history of microfinance investments is short and does not allow an adequate estimation of return, risk and liquidity parameters. Nonetheless, the result exhibits the potential of microfinance investments as a module in strategic asset allocation. Consequently, an analysis with qualitatively derived input parameters might give a more conclusive asset allocation.

6.3.2 Optimization with qualitative microfinance parameters

In this section, the asset allocation optimization with parameters of the scenario workshops is outlined. Hence, scenario results for microfinance debt investments are included into the previously used asset allocation framework.

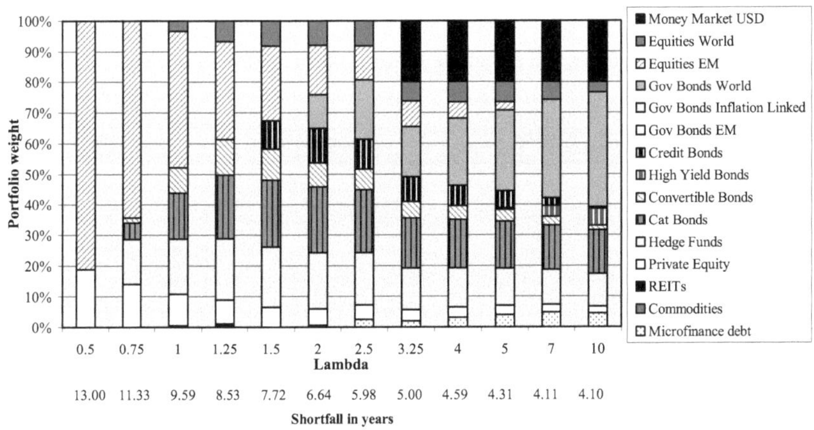

Figure 6-8: Optimized portfolios weights including microfinance (qualitative approach)

Microfinance debt investments have a moderate weight in many portfolios, which mainly correspond to the portfolios without microfinance exposure. In portfolios with a shortfall up to 6 years microfinance debt has a quota of about 2.5-5%. In more aggressive growth portfolios with a shortfall above 7 years, microfinance debt is not added to portfolios. This primarily reflects the lower expected return and higher expected risk of microfinance debt than expressed in purely quantitatively derived parameters. However, it also states the attractiveness of microfinance investments for risk-averse investors. In conclusion, the portfolios are well-balanced between several asset classes and the portfolios with a lower risk-profile have a moderate microfinance weight.

6.4 Implication for asset allocation

6.4.1 Cross-comparison of portfolios

The three sets of portfolio compositions (two with and one without microfinance investments) have different characteristics. A cross-comparison of selected optimized portfolios reveals the differences of portfolios without microfinance, with quantitatively derived microfinance expected parameters and with qualitatively derived microfinance expected parameters (see Figure 6-9).

	lambda 1			lambda 3.25			lambda 7		
	w/o MF	MF quant	MF qual	w/o MF	MF quant	MF qual	w/o MF	MF quant	MF qual
Money Market USD	0.0%	0.0%	0.0%	20.0%	0.0%	20.0%	20.0%	20.0%	20.0%
Equities World	3.4%	0.0%	3.4%	5.5%	3.9%	6.3%	4.0%	2.6%	5.8%
Equities EM	44.5%	47.9%	44.5%	9.2%	10.8%	8.3%	1.7%	3.9%	0.0%
Gov Bonds World	0.0%	0.0%	0.0%	17.9%	3.5%	16.3%	34.2%	15.5%	31.9%
Gov Bonds Inflation Linked	0.0%	0.0%	0.0%	0.0%	0.0%	0.0%	0.0%	0.0%	0.0%
Gov Bonds EM	0.0%	0.0%	0.0%	0.0%	0.0%	0.0%	0.0%	0.0%	0.0%
Credit Bonds	0.0%	0.0%	0.0%	8.3%	6.7%	8.2%	4.2%	4.7%	2.5%
High Yield Bonds	0.0%	0.0%	0.0%	0.0%	0.0%	0.0%	3.9%	0.0%	3.6%
Convertible Bonds	8.4%	0.0%	8.4%	4.9%	5.2%	5.5%	1.8%	2.6%	2.9%
Cat Bonds	15.0%	0.0%	15.0%	16.8%	12.3%	16.3%	15.7%	10.2%	14.4%
Hedge Funds	18.0%	3.7%	18.0%	13.7%	10.6%	13.6%	11.7%	7.9%	11.4%
Private Equity	10.2%	10.6%	10.2%	3.7%	3.2%	3.7%	2.7%	2.1%	2.6%
REITs	0.5%	0.0%	0.6%	0.0%	0.0%	0.0%	0.0%	0.0%	0.0%
Commodities	0.0%	0.0%	0.0%	0.0%	0.0%	0.0%	0.0%	0.0%	0.0%
Microfinance debt	0.0%	37.8%	0.0%	0.0%	43.8%	1.9%	0.0%	30.6%	4.8%
Return p.a.	**8.85%**	**8.68%**	**8.85%**	**5.05%**	**5.77%**	**5.04%**	**4.09%**	**4.39%**	**4.07%**
Risk p.a.	**16.66%**	**15.33%**	**16.66%**	**6.87%**	**7.13%**	**6.86%**	**5.07%**	**4.52%**	**5.02%**
Shortfall in years	**9.59**	**8.44**	**9.59**	**5.01**	**4.13**	**5.00**	**4.16**	**2.86**	**4.11**

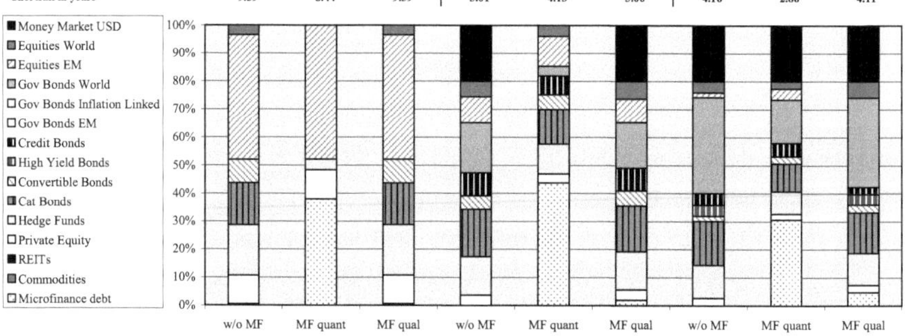

Figure 6-9: Cross-comparison of selected portfolios

The portfolios with a lambda of 1 are exemplary for long-term investors. The portfolio without microfinance holds about 50% in equities with a clear tilt towards emerging markets, another 10% in private equity, close to 20% in hedge funds, 15% in well-diversifying cat bonds and the remaining 8% in convertible bonds. The portfolio has an annual expected return of 8.8% and an annual expected risk of 16.7%. As a consequence, the Telser shortfall with 0% minimum return and a maximum shortfall probability of 5% is about 9.6 years. The introduction of microfinance debt investments based on a standard quantitative approach would change the portfolio allocation extremely. In such a portfolio, microfinance debt has a weight of about 38%, emerging market equities again close to 50%, private equity exposure of 10% and some 4% of hedge fund exposure. The diversifying exposures of cat bonds, convertible bonds and hedge funds are completely or almost completely shifted into microfinance debt investments. As a result, the expected annual return is with 8.7% similar to the portfolio without microfinance. But the expected annual risk is lowered by more than 1% to 15.3% due to the low risk expectation of microfinance debt investments. Therefore the Telser shortfall criteria are expected to be met with a minimum investment period of only 8.5 years. The portfolio with qualitatively derived expected input parameters is identical to the one without microfinance. For long-term investors no microfinance debt investments are recommended from a portfolio theory perspective.

The portfolios with a lambda of 3.25 are exemplary for investors that prefer a growth portfolio with moderate risks. The optimized portfolio without microfinance investments is well-diversified ranging from money market, equities, government bonds, credit and convertible bonds, cat bonds and hedge funds to a small portion of private equity. The expected annualised return is 5.1% and the expected annualised risk 6.9%. As a result, the shortfall constraints are met after an expected investment period of 5 years. Again, the inclusion of microfinance with standard quantitative parameters causes a major shift of the portfolio. More than 40% are invested in microfinance debt mainly at the expense of the money market exposure, government bonds, credit bonds investments and hedge funds. Consequently, the expected return rises to 5.8% per annum and the risk is expected to be 7.1%. Thus, the shortfall is significantly lower than in the portfolio without microfinance. It is reduced by almost one year to about four years. The optimized portfolio with qualitatively derived input parameters during the scenario analysis generates a different allocation. The microfinance debt exposure is comparably moderate with about 2%. This quota is mainly at the expense of government bond and cat bond investments. However, the diversification aspect also leads to a shift from emerging market equity exposure to developed market equity exposure. This makes intuitively sense and is an indication for an adequate covariance matrix. As a consequence, the expected return is 5.0% and the expected risk 6.9%. Hence these parameters and the shortfall of five years are almost identical to the portfolio without microfinance.

The portfolios with a lambda of 7 are exemplary for risk-averse investors. The portfolio without microfinance contains 20% money market exposure, about 35% government bonds, about 8% credit and high yield bonds, 15.7% cat bonds, 11.7% hedge funds and some minor exposure of about 6% to equities and 2.7% to private equity. As a result, an expected return of 4.1% and expected risk of 5.1% apply. The shortfall criteria are met with an investment period of at least 4 years and 2 months. The portfolio calculated with quantitatively obtained microfinance debt investment parameters differs again widely. The microfinance exposure of 30% results mainly at the expense of government bonds world and cat bonds. Overall, the expected return is 4.4% and the expected risk 4.5%. Consequently, the shortfall is more than one year below the shortfall period without microfinance investment. In the portfolio optimized with microfinance input parameters of the scenario analysis, the microfinance quota is comparably moderate with about 5%. This results at the expense of a moderate reduction of government bonds and cat bonds. Some slight shifts in bond exposure result from credit risk to equity risk in convertible bonds. Furthermore, again the equity risk is focused on developed markets. In conclusion, an expected return of 4.1% and an expected risk of 5.0% apply. The resulting shortfall period is with 4.1 years slightly lower than in a portfolio without microfinance investment.

The comparison of the efficient frontiers depicts the portfolio effects of microfinance debt investments. Investors with a high or moderate risk aversion can benefit slightly from a microfinance allocation in their portfolio (see Figure 6-10). Furthermore, the figure shows the extreme overestimation of microfinance debt investments in portfolio theory applying quantitatively derived input parameters. In conclusion, the "scenario analysis microfinance" and the integration into an asset allocation model reveal only very moderate portfolio effects of microfinance debt investments for risk-averse investors with a short- or mid-term investment horizon. Furthermore, the asset allocation modelling exhibits a marked overestimation of microfinance debt investments by standard quantitative approaches.

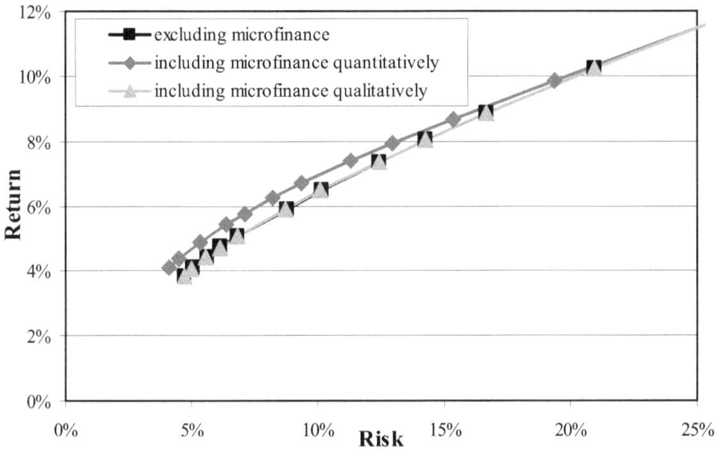

Figure 6-10: Efficient frontiers of portfolios without and with MF debt

6.4.2 Cross-comparison of portfolio backtests

A cross-comparison of portfolio backtests indicates no clear preference of portfolios with or without microfinance. On the one hand, the portfolios without microfinance performed better in the last year (Figure 6-11). However, over the long-term the return differences between the portfolios excluding and including microfinance diminish. On the other hand, microfinance investments reduce the risk of these portfolios slightly. Over the past few years, microfinance debt investments optimized portfolios only for very risk-averse investors. Hence, the shortfall of the lambda 7 and lambda 10 portfolios is in the long-run lower than for the corresponding portfolios without microfinance. But for all other investors (lambda 2-5), microfinance debt investments did not optimize the portfolios in any examined time horizon. Nevertheless, past performance is no indication of future performance. Furthermore, the return and risk expectations as well as liquidity risks associated with other asset classes changed markedly during the past few years. As a consequence, these backtests clearly demonstrate that microfinance investments offer attractive diversification with the limited up- and also downside of hold-to-maturity fixed income products.

		lambda 2		lambda 2.5		lambda 3.25		lambda 4		lambda 5		lambda 7		lambda 10	
		w/o MF	MF qual	w/o MF	MF qual	w/o MF	MF qual	w/o MF	MF qual	w/o MF	MF qual	w/o MF	MF qual	w/o MF	MF qual
-1y	return p.a.	28.4%	28.2%	24.4%	23.9%	19.0%	18.7%	16.7%	16.1%	14.8%	14.0%	12.8%	12.0%	11.4%	10.8%
	risk p.a.	12.9%	12.8%	11.4%	11.3%	9.0%	8.9%	8.2%	8.0%	7.5%	7.3%	6.7%	6.4%	6.2%	5.9%
	shortfall	0.56	0.56	0.60	0.61	0.60	0.60	0.65	0.67	0.70	0.74	0.74	0.79	0.79	0.81
-3y	return p.a.	2.9%	2.8%	3.4%	3.2%	3.2%	3.0%	3.5%	3.3%	3.8%	3.5%	4.2%	3.9%	4.6%	4.5%
	risk p.a.	14.6%	14.6%	12.0%	11.9%	9.1%	9.0%	7.8%	7.7%	6.8%	6.6%	5.8%	5.5%	5.1%	4.9%
	shortfall	71.38	73.24	33.28	36.59	22.33	24.30	13.53	14.98	8.66	9.66	5.04	5.39	3.33	3.16
-5y	return p.a.	5.8%	5.7%	5.4%	5.3%	4.9%	4.8%	4.7%	4.5%	4.5%	4.3%	4.4%	4.2%	4.3%	4.3%
	risk p.a.	9.6%	9.6%	8.2%	8.1%	6.4%	6.4%	5.7%	5.5%	5.1%	4.9%	4.4%	4.2%	4.1%	3.9%
	shortfall	7.52	7.55	6.15	6.26	4.74	4.83	3.99	4.05	3.40	3.45	2.80	2.76	2.42	2.21
-10y	return p.a.	4.5%	4.5%	4.5%	4.4%	4.1%	4.0%	4.1%	4.0%	4.1%	4.0%	4.2%	4.0%	4.3%	4.2%
	risk p.a.	7.8%	7.8%	6.5%	6.5%	5.1%	5.0%	4.5%	4.4%	4.0%	3.9%	3.6%	3.4%	3.4%	3.2%
	shortfall	7.95	7.99	5.63	5.75	4.11	4.16	3.20	3.25	2.57	2.60	1.99	1.97	1.70	1.60

Figure 6-11: Cross-comparison of portfolio backtests without and with MF debt[183]

6.4.3 Implications for investors

The implications of microfinance debt in an asset allocation context are diverging depending on the investor type. In the following, recommendations for the investor categories defined in chapter 2.3 are outlined. These asset allocation recommendations are mainly based on the optimization with qualitatively derived microfinance debt investment input parameters.

Very risk-averse private investor

Microfinance debt investments are a source of return for very risk-averse portfolios. These investors seek for a stable portfolio with capital preservation and in second place growth and final wealth. On the one hand the mixture of emerging market and credit exposure offered by microfinance debt investments diversifies the asset allocation. On the other hand microfinance debt investments offer an expected return more or less equivalent to the expected portfolio return. Moreover, microfinance investments offer an additional social return for the investor. In conclusion, depending on the specific risk-aversion and investment horizon as well as social motivation of an investor the microfinance debt investment exposure is recommended in the range of 2-5% of the investors' portfolio.

[183] The investigated period ends in February 2010. A monthly rebalancing is assumed and returns are calculated from indices stated in Figure 6-1.

Risk-averse wealthy private investor

For risk-averse wealthy private investors' portfolios microfinance debt investments are a source of diversification. These investors aim for a well-diversified portfolio with some growth potential. Microfinance debt investments offer diversification potential. Furthermore, the asset class adds a different return component into the portfolio. On top of this, the investment generates a social return in the emerging markets. This and the increasing popularity of microfinance may generate an additional emotional return for the investor as an interesting topic for discussion in business and private life emerges. In conclusion, depending on the specific risk-aversion and investment horizon as well as social and emotional motivation of an investor, the microfinance debt investment exposure is recommended in the range of 2-4% of the investors' portfolio.

Long-term investing family office

Family offices prefer a long-term growth potential. As a consequence, the portfolio of a family office is very well-diversified in asset classes with high expected returns. This includes equities, the more risky bonds categories such as high yield bonds and convertible bonds as well as cat bonds, hedge funds for diversification and private equity investments. Standard microfinance debt investments are not a reasonable asset class. However, microfinance debt funds with non-hedged local currency exposure offer a higher return potential and access to otherwise non-investable exposures. Furthermore, the investment in microfinance equity as a portion of the private equity quota opens up further broadly untapped investments. As a consequence, microfinance is not a standard investment for family offices. Nevertheless in some niches attractive investments may arise, but funds and investable products are very limited.

Pension fund

Microfinance debt investments are not a preferred asset class per se for pension funds. Due to the illiquidity combined with the moderate return potential, the attractiveness for liquidity and return-seeking pension funds is limited. However, in several countries investment restrictions and guidelines with a social component apply. These constraints may in some cases make a microfinance debt investment reasonable. In conclusion, unless social and sustainable guidelines apply microfinance debt investments are not fitting into a pension funds asset allocation.

State investment fund

The very long-term investment horizon of sovereign wealth funds does not correspond with the benefits of microfinance debt investments. Hence, standard microfinance investments are not attractive. However, high risk local currency exposure or microfinance equity investments may offer an attractive return potential. Moreover, a political interest in the microfinance sector of the own or some partner countries can also be a reason for an allocation. In general, despite political interest or very specific high risk exposures microfinance investments are not attractive for state investment funds.

6.4.4 Microfinance investment limitations

A further limiting factor for investments in microfinance is the market size. As mentioned, the volume of foreign equity and debt investments is currently about USD 6.5 billion. Therefore, a broad shift of private and institutional investors is impossible. For example, the whole microfinance market open for foreign investments is about a tenth of Bill Gates' wealth, about 5% of a medium-size private bank's assets under management or less than 0.5% of the biggest wealth managers' assets under management. In conclusion, microfinance investments are an asset allocation solution for smart private investors and not a product for the mass market. From an asset allocation perspective the attractiveness for big institutional investors is even further reduced by the small market volume as no reasonable exposure can be taken.

6.5 Summary

Microfinance debt investments optimize portfolios of risk-averse investors. The moderate correlation and paired with an attractive fixed income risk-return profile make microfinance debt investments favourable for risk averse private investors. The emerging market exposure with a relatively low risk and the fast adaptation to change in interest rates are two suitable key characteristics for balanced portfolios with a lower risk budget. As a result, an exposure of 2-5% for risk-averse private investors is recommended. Investors with a higher risk budget might prefer local currency microfinance debt exposure or even private equity-like investments in microfinance equity. However, investors should take liquidity constraints and the limited markets size into account.

7 Conclusion

7.1 Summary of results

Microfinance is an interesting asset class with a double bottom line. Social as well as financial returns can be generated and therefore fit in today's time as many institutional and private investors seek for sustainable investments. Up to now, a single digit billion market size indicates that the market is not mature. However, firstly it is growing tremendously. Secondly, for strategic asset allocation purposes also small asset categories can be considered and emerge with investors' money. A perfect example for this is the cat bond market with about USD 16 billion currently outstanding.

A major difficulty is the inexperience of investors and the short investment history of microfinance. Microfinance debt investment vehicles broadly diversify across countries and microfinance institutions. However, the underlying risk is a credit portfolio of small enterprise loans in emerging markets. The assessment of return and risk parameters proves to be difficult, standard credit screening processes of rating agencies such as Fitch or Standard & Poor's are not convincing yet. Furthermore, the risks and mission of microfinance credits may shift with the evolution of the asset class. Thus, also new risks may affect investments.

The results of the quantitative approach in this study demonstrate the potential of microfinance in a strategic asset allocation framework, but the validity of results is questionable. Despite a high illiquidity discount, microfinance debt investments dominate the optimized model portfolios with up to 45%. As discussed, the derivation of risk and return parameters is problematic, because past evidence is scarce and does not include many economic regimes or innovation potential. This is a typical problem set of a young, emerging asset class.

The theoretical concept outlined in this study to address such a problem set is scenario planning, which is practically proven in various fields. A structured scenario process with expertise of all involved fields generates relevant information and development perspectives of a new asset class. Hence, a qualitative approach such as scenario analysis extends the capabilities of a quantitative asset allocation context.

The conducted scenario analysis on microfinance demonstrates chances and risks of the two asset classes: microfinance debt and microfinance equity. The process was led by scenario experts from Daimler AG and the participants included well-known specialists from microfinance as well as emerging market and asset allocation senior professionals from LGT CM. The scenario analysis was realised in various pre-meetings, two two-day off-sites with all participants and a closing day. During the process the team developed several scenarios for microfinance and assessed the impact on microfinance debt and equity investments. As a result, the qualitative process reveals a difference in the return profile of microfinance debt investments compared to a common quantitative analysis. Moreover a return estimate for microfinance equity investments is generated. In addition, the scenario analysis determines a higher correlation and risk of microfinance investments than currently expected by most market participants and quantitative analysis. As a consequence, the process unveils a different picture of microfinance investments than a common quantitative analysis of past performances would demonstrate.

The integration of the results of the microfinance scenario analysis into an asset allocation framework reveals only a very slight attractiveness of microfinance debt investments. It discloses the overestimation of this asset class by a common quantitative assessment. According to performed portfolio optimizations with qualitatively derived input parameters, microfinance debt investments are slightly attractive for risk-averse investors. An addition of about 2-5% microfinance debt exposure is suggested. For institutional and return seeking investors the volume of the asset class and the return potential limit the attractiveness. However, local currency microfinance debt and microfinance equity investments offer a higher return potential. But up to now investment possibilities in these specific asset categories are very limited. These results are reasonable from a practitioner's point of view, but they stand in contrast to portfolio optimizations with quantitatively derived input parameters that recommend a microfinance debt exposure of up to 45%. In conclusion, microfinance debt investments improve the return/risk pattern of an investment portfolio and shift the efficient frontier slightly to the left.

7.2 Outlook and implications

Asset allocation and scenario methodologies intertwine perfectly. In the specific case of a new asset class this study demonstrates that the qualitative approach of a scenario process captures more relevant information also regarding asset allocation as opposed to a common quantitative approach. Furthermore, the forward-looking character of this approach generates asset allocation input parameters in the required forward-looking dimension. In contrast to this, quantitative models cannot overcome the problem of extrapolating estimates from past data. This allows by definition no innovation or mission drift and assumes that all relevant scenario information is included in the past data series. As a result, a well-structured qualitative approach to generate asset allocation input parameter dominates quantitative approaches.

A qualitative methodology is a key instrument for the integration of young asset classes into an asset allocation context. Firstly, the process develops a deeper understanding of the asset class and takes several perspectives for an assessment into consideration. Secondly, a comprehensive set of asset allocation input parameters can be derived with a forward-looking perspective. The innovative character, a possible mission drift and several potential futures are analysed and allow a profound evaluation. In conclusion, a qualitative approach such as scenario methodologies is a rational way to assess emerging asset classes. The problematic quantitative evaluations of newly structured products as seen in the last decade are an indication for this.

Scenario analysis is a comprehensive tool to close the gaps of the quantitative assessments for asset allocation purposes and generate an added value. However, a scenario process also has to cope with the limitations of a team process such as motivation or political issues. Furthermore a scenario analysis is a time-consuming and hence costly approach. But for the same reasons, the decisions that are made have the common basis of all participants and are a reasoned assessment. In conclusion, a scenario process is an adequate assessment tool both for new asset classes and also for mature ones.

This study shows that quantitatively driven asset allocation can be problematic. A qualitative assessment of asset classes with scenario methodologies is an adequate supplement to quantitative approaches in asset allocation. It enhances the quality of as well as the trust in asset allocation parameters. However, performing scenario approaches for all asset classes is very time-consuming and costly. Thus, a focus on selected asset classes is advisable. The criteria to select asset classes for an additional qualitative analysis with scenario methodologies are innovation or mission drift, illiquidity and desired knowledge transfer for participants. As discussed, a new pattern of an asset class cannot be captured in quantitative analysis. The increase of government debt in many countries following the credit crises might be such a turning point in the government bond market. Illiquid asset classes cannot be traded at any time. Furthermore some investments such as private equity or forest investments are taken for 7-20 years and the secondary market is small. Consequently, illiquid asset classes such as private equity, hedge funds and the small but very attractive asset class cat bonds qualify for a scenario analysis. Additionally, investors' know-how regarding these asset classes is often limited and can be increased throughout the scenario process. As a result, a scenario approach is recommended for hedge fund and private equity investments due to the asset class characteristics. Moreover, the current economic environment advises an analysis of the government bond market.

In conclusion, an adequate consideration of the magic triangle of asset allocation – namely return, risk and liquidity estimates – can be applied with an intertwined approach of qualitative and quantitative assessment methodologies.

Bibliography

Auckenthaler, C. (1991). *Trust Banking – Theorie und Praxis des Anlagegeschäfts.* Bern: Paul Haupt.

Bank for International Settlements (BIS, 2005). *Amendment to the Capital Accord to incorporate market risks.* Retrieved December 14, 2009 from http://www.bis.org/publ/bcbs119.pdf?noframes=1

Bank for International Settlements (BIS, 2004). *International Convergence of Capital Measurement and Capital Standards.* Retrieved December 14, 2009 from http://www.bis.org/publ/bcbs107.pdf

Barclays Capital (2010). *Global family of indices – February 2010.* Retrieved March 12, 2010 from www.themarkets.com (restricted access).

BlueOrchard (2009). *Fund prospect Dexia Microcredit Fund.* Retrieved May 14, 2009 from http://www.blueorchard.com/jahia/Jahia/Products_1/pid/190

Brinson, G. P., Hood, L. R. & G. L. Beebower (1986). Determinants of Portfolio Performance. *Financial Analysts Journal*, 39-44.

Brooks, C. & H. M. Kat (2002). The Statistical Properties of Hedge Fund Return Index Returns and Their Implications for Investors. *The Journal of Alternative Investments*, 26-44.

Callaghan, I., Gonazalez, H. Maurice, D. & C. Novak (2007). Microfinance – On the Road to Capital Markets. *Journal of Applied Corporate Finance*, Morgan Stanley, 115-124.

Campbell, J. Y., Lo, A. W. & A. C. MacKinlay (1997). *The econometrics of financial markets*. Princeton: Princeton University Press

Citigroup (2010). *International market indexes – February 2010 performance.* Retrieved March 12, 2010 from www.themarkets.com (restricted access).

Consultative Group to Assist the Poor (CGAP, 2009a). *The impact of the financial crisis on microfinance institutions and their clients.* CGAP Brief. Retrieved December 14, 2009 from http://www.cgap.org/gm/document-1.9.38570/CGAPBrief_MIV.pdf

Consultative Group to Assist the Poor (CGAP, 2009b). *MIV performance and prospects: highlights from the CGAP 2009 MIV Benchmark Survey.* CGAP Brief. Retrieved December 14, 2009 from http://www.cgap.org/gm/document-1.9.38570/CGAPBrief_MIV.pdf

Consultative Group to Assist the Poor (CGAP, 2009c). *Asset and liability management for deposit-taking microfinance institutions.* CGAP focus note. Retrieved December 14, 2009 from http://www.cgap.org/gm/document-1.9.34818/FN55.pdf

Consultative Group to Assist the Poor (CGAP, 2007). *Savings for poor people: good for clients, good for business?* Retrieved December 14, 2009 from http://dev.cgap.org/gm/document-1.9.3912/Portfolio_Dec2007.pdf

Chobra, V. & W. Ziemba (1993). The effects of errors in means, variances, and covariances on optimal portfolio choice. *Journal of Portfolio Management*, 6 -11.

Churchill, C. (2006). *What is insurance for the poor.* In Churchill, C. (ed.), Protecting the poor: a microinsurance compendium, ILO, 12-24.

Coleman, J. (1990). Social capital in the creation of human capital. *American Journal of Sociology*, 95-120.

Copeland, T. E. & J. E. Weston (1988). *Financial theory and corporate policy*, 3rd ed. Reading: Addison Wesley.

Credit Suisse First Boston (2010). *CSFB/Tremont Hedge Fund Index*, www.hedgeindex.com.

Davies, G. (2004). *Scenarios come to Davos. A GBN conversation with Ged Davis.* Retrieved December 12, 2009 from http://www.weforum.org/pdf/CSI/GBN_Davis_interview.pdf

Dieckmann, R. (2007). *Microfinance: an emerging investment opportunity.* International Issues. Frankfurt: Deutsche Bank Research.

EFSE (2010). *Microcredit for big ideas.* EFSE brochure. Retrieved February 2, 2010 from http://www.efse.lu/fileadmin/downloads/publications/brochures/EFSE_Microcredit.pdf

Fama, E. & K. R. French (1993). Common risk factors in the returns on stocks and bonds. *Journal of Financial Economics*, 3-56.

Fama, E. (1965). The behaviour of stock market prices. *Journal of Business*, 34-105.

Felder-Kozu, N. (2008). *Kleiner Einsatz, grosse Wirkung. Mikrofinanzierung und Mikrofranchising – Modelle gegen die Armut.* Zürich: rüffer & rub.

Gantenbein, P. Laternser, S. & K. Spremann (2001). *Anlageberatung und Portofoliomanagement.* Zürich: NZZ Verlag.

Gottschalk, K. & M. Steinbrecher (2005). Wie Szenarien die strategische Unternehmenssteuerung balancieren. *Organisationsentwicklung,* 24-33.

GPR (2009). *GPR construction and maintenance procedures. FTSE NAREIT US real estate index series.* Retrieved January 14, 2010 from http://www.propertyshares.com/images/pdf/ConstructionMaintenanceSeptember2006.pdf

Hollis, A. & A. Sweetman (2003). *Microfinance and Famine: The Irish Loan Funds during the Great Famine.* Working Paper.

Hollis, A. & A. Sweetman (1997). *Complementarity, Competition and Institutional Development: The Irish Loan Funds through Three Centuries.* Working Paper.

Horneff, W.J., Raimond, H. M., Mitchell, O. S. & M. Z. Stamos (2009). Asset allocation over the life cycle with investment-linked survival-contingent payouts. *Journal of Banking and Finance*, 1688-1699.

J.P.Morgan (2010). *Emerging markets bond index monitor.* Retrieved March 12, 2010 from www.themarkets.com (restricted access).

Kaduff, J. V. (1996). *Shortfall-risk-basierte Portfolio-Strategien: Grundlagen, Anwendungen, Algorithmen.* Bern: Paul Haupt.

Kalin, D. & R. Zagst (1999). Portfolio optimization: volatility constraints versus shortfall constraints. *OR Spectrum*, 97-122.

Kataoka, S. (1963). A stochastic programming model. *Econometrica*, 181-196.

Kielholz, W. & A. P. Durrer (1997). Insurance derivatives and securitization: new hedging perspectives for the US cat insurance market. *The Geneva Papers on Risk and Insurance*, 3-16.

Lang, S. (2009). *Core Satellite Portfoliomanagement.* Bern: Haupt Verlag.

Lhabitant, F. S. (2004). *Hedge funds – quantitative insights.* Chichester: Wiley.

Lintner, J. (1965). The valuation of risk assets and the selection of risky investments in stock portfolios and capital budgets. *Review of Economics and Statistics*, 13-37.

Littlefield, E. & C. Kneiding (2009). *The global financial crisis and its impact on microfinance.* CGAP Occasional Paper.

LPX (2009). *Guide to the LPX equity indices*, Version 2.7. Retrieved January 14, 2010 from http://www.lpx-group.com/lpx/fileadmin/images/indices/ LPX_ Guide_to_the_Equity_Indices.pdf

Mandelbrot, B. (1963). New methods in statistical economics. *Journal of Political Economy*, 207-209.

Markowitz, H. (1987). *Mean-variance analysis.* Oxford: Basil Blackwell.

Markowitz, H. (1959). *Portfolio Selection – Efficient Diversification of Investments.* New York: John Wiley.

Markowitz, H. (1952). Portfolio Selection. *Journal of Finance*, 77-91.

Maslakovic, M. (2009). *IFSL report on sovereign wealth funds 2009.* Retrieved December 28, 2009 from http://www.ifsl.org.uk/upload/CBS_Sovereign %20Wealth%20Funds%202009.pdf

McKinsey (2006). *Optimising capital supply in support of microfinance industry growth.* Presentation for Omidyar Network/The SEEP Network, Microfinance Investor Roundtable. Retrieved August 24, 2009 from http://seepstage. forumone.com/content/library/detail/4656

Meehan, J. (2004). *Tapping financial markets for microfinance.* Working Paper. Retrieved August 25, 2009 from http://www.microcapital.org/downloads/ resourcepapers/GFUSA-CapitalMarkets.pdf

Merton, R. C. (1990). *Continuous-time finance.* Cambridge: Blackwell.

Merton, R. C. (1969). Lifetime portfolio selection under uncertainty: the continuous time case. *Review of Economics and Statistics*, 247-257.

Minx, E. & E. Böhlke (2006). Denken in alternativen Zukünften. *Internationale Politik* Nr. 12, 14-22.

Minx, E. & H. Roehl (2006). Werkzeugkiste für Berater und Change Manager: 9. Szenario-Technik. *Organisationsentwicklung*, 78-81.

Minx, E. & H. Roehl (1998). Von Inseln und Brücken – Wissensentwicklung durch Szenarien bei der Daimler-Benz AG. *zfo* no.3, 167-170.

Missler-Behr, M. (2006). *Auf der Suche nach Zukunftsbildern – eine Regelbasis zur Szenarienauswahl.* In: Wilms, F. (eds.). Szenariotechnik. Vom Umgang mit der Zukunft. Bern: Paul Haupt.

MIX/Microfinance Information Exchange (2009). *The MicroBanking Bulleting No. 19.* Retrieved January 16, 2010 from http://www.themix.org/sites/ default/files/MBB%2019%20-%20December%202009_0.pdf

MIX/Microfinance Information Exchange (2008). *The MicroBanking Bulleting No. 17.* Retrieved January 16, 2009 from http://www.themix.org/microbanking-bulletin/mbb-issue-no-17-autumn-2008

Mossin, J. (1966). Equilibrium in a capital asset market. *Econometrica*, 768-783.

MSCI Barra (2010). *Index definitions*. Retrieved March 12, 2010 from http://www.mscibarra.com/products/indices/international_equity_indices/definitions.html

Porter, M. (1985). *Competitive Advantage.* New York: Free Press.

Reilly, F. K. & K. C. Brown (2006). *Investment analysis and portfolio management*, 8th edition. Mason: Thomson.

responsAbility (2009). *Fund prospect responsAbility Global MF Fund.* Retreived May 14, 2009 from http://www.responsability.com/site/index.cfm?id_art=42157&act MenuItemID=20541&vsprache=DE

Ringland, G. (1998). *Scenario planning*. Managing for the future. Chichester: Wiley & Sons.

Ringland, G. (2002). *Scenarios in business*. Chichester: Wiley & Sons.

Rosenberg, R., Gonzalez, A. & S. Narain (2009). *The New Moneylenders: Are the Poor Being Exploited by High Microcredit Interest Rates?* CGAP Occasional Paper.

Roy, A. D. (1952). Safety first and the holding of assets. *Econometrica,* 431-449.

Scholes, M. & J. Williams (1977). Estimating betas from nonsynchronous data. *Journal of Financial Economics*, 309-327.

SWP (Stiftung Wissenschaft und Politik, 2008). *Europäische Energiesicherheit 2020. Szenarien für mögliche Entwicklungen in Europa und seinen energiepolitisch wichtigsten Nachbarregionen.* SWP-Studien.

Schwartz, P. (1996). *The art of the long view: paths to strategic insight for yourself and your company*. New York: Doubleday.

Seibel, H. D. (2005). *Does history matter? The old and the new world of microfinance in Europe and Asia.* Working Paper.

Seibel, H. D. (2003). *History matters in microfinance*. Working Paper.

Sharpe, W. F., Alexander, G. J. & J. V. Bailey (1999). *Investments*, 6th ed. Upper Saddle River: Prentice Hall.

Sharpe, W. F. (1964). Capital asset prices: a theory of market equilibrium under conditions of risk. *Journal of Finance*, 425-442.

Standard & Poor's (2009). *S&P GSCI commodity indices*. Retrieved on January 14, 2010 from http://www2.standardandpoors.com/spf/pdf/index/SP_GSCI_ Factsheet.pdf

Steiner, M. & C. Bruns (2007). *Wertpapiermanagement*, 9th ed. Stuttgart: Schäffer-Poeschel.

Spremann, K. & P. Gantenbein (2005). *Kapitalmärkte.* Stuttgart: Lucius&Lucius.

Spremann, K. (2008). *Portfoliomanagement*, 4th ed. München: Oldenbourg.

Spremann, K. (1997). Humankapital im Portefeuille privater Investoren. *Zeitschrift für Betriebswirtschaft*, 145-147.

Spremann, K. (1995). *Asset-Allokation im Lebenszyklus und Vintage-Programm.* In: Gehrig, G. (eds.): Private Banking, Zürich, 115-146.

Swiss Re (2007). *Swiss Re launches the first catastrophe bond indices*. Retrieved January 14, 2010 from http://www.swissre.com/resources /a67d68804660790fb 923fd276a9800c6-IDUR_74LC9G_Swis.pdf

Symbiotics (2010). *Symbiotics50 index information.* Retrieved February 14, 2010 from Symbiotics (restricted access).

Telser, L. G. (1955). Safety first and hedging. *The Review of Economic Studies*, 1-16.

Treynor, J. (1962). *Toward a theory of market value of risky assets*. Unpublished manuscript.

Tobin (1965). *The theory of portfolio selecting.* Brechling, F.B.R & Hahn, F.H. (editors). The theory of interest rates. London: Macmillan.

UBS (2008). *UBS global convertible bond index. Index guidelines*. Retrieved on March 12, 2010 from www.themarkets.com (restricted access).

Uysal, E., Trainer, F. H. & J. Reiss (2001). Revisiting mean-variance optimization. *Journal of Portfolio Management*, 71-81.

von Pischke, J. D. (2006). *New partnerships for sustainability and outreach.* In Matthäus-Maier, I. & von Pischke, J.D. (eds.), New partnerships for innovation in microfinance (pp. 1-13). Berlin: Springer.

von Stauffenberg, D. (2008). *The 2007 microfinance investment vehicle survey.* Retrieved February 28, 2009 from http://microrate.com/home/publications/microfinance-research-reports

Wack, P. (1985). Scenarios: shooting the rapids. *Harvard Business Review*, 139-150.

Wack, P. (1985). Scenarios: unchartered waters ahead. *Harvard Business Review*, 72-79.

WEF Report (2010). *The future of the global financial system - navigating the challenges ahead.* World Scenario Series. Retrieved February 2, 2010 from http://www.weforum.org/en/initiatives/Scenarios/NFA/index.htm

WEF Report (2009a). *The Future of the global financial system: a near-term outlook and long-term scenarios.* World Scenario Series. Retrieved March 13, 2009 from http://www.weforum.org/en/initiatives/Scenarios/NewFinancialArchitecture/index.htm

WEF (2009b). *Scenario planning*. Homepage of World Economic Forum. Retrieved April 16, 2009 from http://www.weforum.org/en/initiatives/Scenarios/index.htm

Zimmermann, H. (2004). Sind Kapitalschutzstrategien in der Vorsorge sinnvoll? Überlegungen aus ökonomischer Sicht. *Schweizer Personalvorsorge*, 19-25.

Interviews

De Bleecker, Berg. PGGM, Investment Manager. Telephone interview. Amsterdam: June 30, 2009.

Huber, Patrik. responsAbility Social Investments AG, Member of the Board. Personal interview. Zurich: April 28, 2009 and several more discussions during and after the scenario process.

Krauss, Annette. University of Zurich, Head of Centre for Microfinance. Personal interview. Zurich: April 2, 2009 and several more discussions during the scenario process.

Knöpfel, Ivo. onValues, CEO. Personal interview. Zurich: June 26, 2009.

Mammertz, Rochus. responsAbility Social Investments AG, equity and regulation specialist. Telephone interview. Zurich: June 30, 2009.

von Stauffenberg, Damian. Microrate, CEO. Personal interview. London: October 31, 2008 and several more discussions during the scenario process.

Appendix

Appendix– 1: Descriptor essay no. 12 – market structure in MFI segment

Scenario analysis microfinance Workshop II

Market structure in MFI segment		12
Projection A:	*Strong consolidation*	*20%*
Projection B:	*Moderate consolidation*	*70%*
Projection C:	*Fragmentation*	*10%*

Definition	The factor market structure in MFI segment describes the concentration of MFIs and the resulting competition and business volume.
Indicators	• MFIs/volume • # of MFI startups • # of MFI closures • # of MFI M&A
Status-quo	The microfinance market is currently fragmented. In most countries and regions, several MFIs offer their product. However, in some markets such as Indonesia or Bangladesh monopolistic structures exist. Up to now, regulatory guidelines fostered fragmentation. But the financial crises clarifies, that the regulation and control of less MFIs is aspired. Moreover, fragmentation was supported by NGO-MFIs, which are dependent on donations. These financial means have become harder to get during the crisis. In addition, the market structure suffers from a complex ownership structure of most MFIs. Thus in several countries and regions a consolidation is difficult.

Storyline of projections	
Projection A	More and more the financial markets took part in the microfinance business. However, they preferred major MFIs as investment objectives and partners. These were able to make use of innovations such as "mobile banking". Furthermore major players created more synergies in credit assessment, back-office processes in general, client management and also funding. In addition, the authorities regulated the market entry in several countries from 2010 on. As a result, MFIs were easier to monitor for the authorities. In 2015, in most countries the MFI market is now consolidated and only a few major market players exist.
Projection B	MFIs were increasingly funded by capital markets and deposits. For an efficient service, both funding sources required a certain size of MFIs. However, the complex ownership structures hindered a wave of consolidation. Many socially motivated owners were not convinced of an open market system. However, in the following years the liberal and major MFIs increase and consolidations set in automatically. In 2015, the market is now partially consolidated with several major market-oriented players and many socially motivated NGO-MFIs.
Projection C	The funding sources of MFIs became mainly focused on social returns. Investors requested explicitly a clear outline of the social impact of their financial investments. As a result, locally oriented MFIs became favored as they were able to give a more detailed insight into their clients business. Furthermore, MFIs with an NGO background gained attention again and from 2012 onwards these had by far the best growth rates in the microfinance segment. As a consequence, the market is now (in 2015) in a moderate fragmentation mode.

Appendix– 2: Questionnaire regarding attractiveness of asset classes

Scenario analysis microfinance Workshop II

Questionnaire: RETURN EXPECTATIONS Name: ____________________

Task: ***Please indicate for the following asset classes in every scenario a risk-adjusted attractivity. In which asset class do you want to invest your money?***

Skale:
1 (very unattractive)
2 (unattractive)
3 (rather unattractive)
4 (rather attractive)
5 (attractive)
6 (very attractive)
Joker: - (no answer)

Asset class	Scenario A2	Scenario A3	Scenario A4	Scenario B1	Scenario Wildcard
• MF Equity					
• MF Debt					
• EM Corporate Debt					
• EM Sovereign Debt					
• EM Equity					
• Money Market USD					
• Global Equity					
• Global Bonds					
• High-Yield Bonds					
• Investment Grade Bonds					

Task 2: Please indicate a probability for every scenario
Remark: The probabilities of all five scenarios should add to 100%.

	Scenario A2	Scenario A3	Scenario A4	Scenario B1	Scenario Wildcard
Probability					

Appendix– 3: Questionnaire regarding correlation measures

Scenario analysis microfinance Workshop II

Questionnarie: CORRELATION Name: ______________________

Idea: Measure correlations of macroeconomic and market factors with different asset classes

Factor	**Asset class**	1	0.5	0	-0.5	-1	no answer
• Increasing EM growth	EM Corporate Bonds	☐	☐	☐	☐	☐	☐
	EM Bonds	☐	☐	☐	☐	☐	☐
	EM Equity	☐	☐	☐	☐	☐	☐
	MF Debt	☐	☐	☐	☐	☐	☐
	MF Equity	☐	☐	☐	☐	☐	☐
• Increasing EM inflation	EM Corporate Bonds	☐	☐	☐	☐	☐	☐
	EM Bonds	☐	☐	☐	☐	☐	☐
	EM Equity	☐	☐	☐	☐	☐	☐
	MF Debt	☐	☐	☐	☐	☐	☐
	MF Equity	☐	☐	☐	☐	☐	☐
• Increasing EM FX volatility	EM Corporate Bonds	☐	☐	☐	☐	☐	☐
	EM Bonds	☐	☐	☐	☐	☐	☐
	EM Equity	☐	☐	☐	☐	☐	☐
	MF Debt	☐	☐	☐	☐	☐	☐
	MF Equity	☐	☐	☐	☐	☐	☐
• Increasing global liquidity	EM Corporate Bonds	☐	☐	☐	☐	☐	☐
	EM Bonds	☐	☐	☐	☐	☐	☐
	EM Equity	☐	☐	☐	☐	☐	☐
	MF Debt	☐	☐	☐	☐	☐	☐
	MF Equity	☐	☐	☐	☐	☐	☐
• Increasing political stability (in countries)	EM Corporate Bonds	☐	☐	☐	☐	☐	☐
	EM Bonds	☐	☐	☐	☐	☐	☐
	EM Equity	☐	☐	☐	☐	☐	☐
	MF Debt	☐	☐	☐	☐	☐	☐
	MF Equity	☐	☐	☐	☐	☐	☐
• High debt level	EM Corporate Bonds	☐	☐	☐	☐	☐	☐
	EM Bonds	☐	☐	☐	☐	☐	☐
	EM Equity	☐	☐	☐	☐	☐	☐
	MF Debt	☐	☐	☐	☐	☐	☐
	MF Equity	☐	☐	☐	☐	☐	☐
• Negative primary budget	EM Corporate Bonds	☐	☐	☐	☐	☐	☐
	EM Bonds	☐	☐	☐	☐	☐	☐
	EM Equity	☐	☐	☐	☐	☐	☐
	MF Debt	☐	☐	☐	☐	☐	☐
	MF Equity	☐	☐	☐	☐	☐	☐
• Increasing commodity prices	EM Corporate Bonds	☐	☐	☐	☐	☐	☐
	EM Bonds	☐	☐	☐	☐	☐	☐
	EM Equity	☐	☐	☐	☐	☐	☐
	MF Debt	☐	☐	☐	☐	☐	☐
	MF Equity	☐	☐	☐	☐	☐	☐
• Increasing global political stability	EM Corporate Bonds	☐	☐	☐	☐	☐	☐
	EM Bonds	☐	☐	☐	☐	☐	☐
	EM Equity	☐	☐	☐	☐	☐	☐
	MF Debt	☐	☐	☐	☐	☐	☐
	MF Equity	☐	☐	☐	☐	☐	☐
• Increasing acceptance of market economy in EM	EM Corporate Bonds	☐	☐	☐	☐	☐	☐
	EM Bonds	☐	☐	☐	☐	☐	☐
	EM Equity	☐	☐	☐	☐	☐	☐
	MF Debt	☐	☐	☐	☐	☐	☐
	MF Equity	☐	☐	☐	☐	☐	☐
• Globalisation	EM Corporate Bonds	☐	☐	☐	☐	☐	☐
	EM Bonds	☐	☐	☐	☐	☐	☐
	EM Equity	☐	☐	☐	☐	☐	☐
	MF Debt	☐	☐	☐	☐	☐	☐
	MF Equity	☐	☐	☐	☐	☐	☐

Appendix– 4: Covariance and correlation matrices excluding microfinance

	MM USD	EQ World	EQ EM	FI World	FI IL	FI EM	FI CRE	FI HY	FI CB	FI CAT	HF	PE	REITs	COM
Money Market USD	0.0000	0.0000	0.0000	-0.0001	0.0000	0.0000	0.0000	0.0000	0.0000	0.0000	0.0001	0.0002	0.0000	0.00[illegible]1
Equities World	0.0000	0.0323	0.0398	0.0020	0.0063	0.0115	0.0078	0.0149	0.0195	0.0012	0.0073	0.0384	0.0310	0.01[illegible]1
Equities EM	0.0000	0.0398	0.0659	0.0016	0.0080	0.0176	0.0107	0.0218	0.0269	0.0017	0.0117	0.0542	0.0395	0.02[illegible]9
Gov Bonds World	0.0000	0.0020	0.0016	0.0049	0.0043	0.0022	0.0037	0.0013	0.0025	0.0003	0.0005	-0.0024	0.0040	0.00[illegible]3
Gov Bonds Inflation Linked	-0.0001	0.0063	0.0080	0.0043	0.0076	0.0044	0.0057	0.0047	0.0056	0.0007	0.0020	0.0038	0.0098	0.00[illegible]9
Gov Bonds EM	0.0000	0.0115	0.0176	0.0022	0.0044	0.0121	0.0055	0.0096	0.0093	0.0008	0.0037	0.0156	0.0137	0.00[illegible]6
Credit Bonds	0.0000	0.0078	0.0107	0.0037	0.0057	0.0055	0.0082	0.0069	0.0072	0.0008	0.0026	0.0078	0.0118	0.00[illegible]5
High Yield Bonds	0.0000	0.0149	0.0218	0.0013	0.0047	0.0096	0.0069	0.0166	0.0115	0.0013	0.0047	0.0208	0.0183	0.01[illegible]
Convertible Bonds	0.0000	0.0195	0.0269	0.0025	0.0056	0.0093	0.0072	0.0115	0.0213	0.0013	0.0070	0.0250	0.0178	0.014[illegible]
Cat Bonds	0.0000	0.0012	0.0017	0.0003	0.0007	0.0008	0.0008	0.0013	0.0013	0.0151	0.0007	0.0019	0.0018	0.00[illegible]
Hedge Funds	0.0000	0.0073	0.0117	0.0005	0.0020	0.0037	0.0026	0.0047	0.0070	0.0007	0.0200	0.0121	0.0065	0.00[illegible]
Private Equity	0.0001	0.0384	0.0542	-0.0024	0.0038	0.0156	0.0078	0.0208	0.0250	0.0019	0.0121	0.1307	0.0408	0.02[illegible]
REITs	0.0002	0.0310	0.0395	0.0040	0.0098	0.0137	0.0118	0.0183	0.0178	0.0018	0.0065	0.0408	0.0500	0.020[illegible]
Commodities	0.0000	0.0181	0.0299	0.0023	0.0089	0.0076	0.0085	0.0110	0.0148	0.0018	0.0082	0.0275	0.0207	0.070[illegible]
Risk	**0.5%**	**18.0%**	**25.7%**	**7.0%**	**8.7%**	**11.0%**	**9.1%**	**12.9%**	**14.6%**	**12.3%**	**14.1%**	**36.2%**	**22.4%**	**26.6%**

	MM USD	EQ World	EQ EM	FI World	FI IL	FI EM	FI CRE	FI HY	FI CB	FI CAT	HF	PE	REITs	COM
Money Market USD	1.00	0.01	-0.01	-0.08	-0.04	0.00	-0.04	-0.04	0.00	0.01	0.04	0.06	0.02	0.0[illegible]
Equities World	0.01	1.00	0.86	0.16	0.40	0.58	0.48	0.64	0.75	0.06	0.29	0.59	0.77	0.3[illegible]
Equities EM	0.01	0.86	1.00	0.09	0.36	0.62	0.46	0.66	0.72	0.05	0.32	0.58	0.69	0.4[illegible]
Gov Bonds World	-0.03	0.16	0.09	1.00	0.71	0.29	0.58	0.14	0.25	0.03	0.05	-0.09	0.25	0.1[illegible]
Gov Bonds Inflation Linked	-0.07	0.40	0.36	0.71	1.00	0.46	0.72	0.41	0.44	0.07	0.16	0.12	0.51	0.3[illegible]
Gov Bonds EM	-0.03	0.58	0.62	0.29	0.46	1.00	0.55	0.68	0.58	0.06	0.24	0.39	0.56	0.2[illegible]
Credit Bonds	0.00	0.48	0.46	0.58	0.72	0.55	1.00	0.59	0.55	0.07	0.20	0.24	0.58	0.3[illegible]
High Yield Bonds	-0.03	0.64	0.66	0.14	0.41	0.68	0.59	1.00	0.61	0.08	0.26	0.45	0.64	0.3[illegible]
Convertible Bonds	-0.03	0.75	0.72	0.25	0.44	0.58	0.55	0.61	1.00	0.07	0.34	0.47	0.55	0.38
Cat Bonds	0.00	0.06	0.05	0.03	0.07	0.06	0.07	0.08	0.07	1.00	0.04	0.04	0.06	0.06
Hedge Funds	0.01	0.29	0.32	0.05	0.16	0.24	0.20	0.26	0.34	0.04	1.00	0.24	0.21	0.2[illegible]
Private Equity	0.01	0.59	0.58	-0.09	0.12	0.39	0.24	0.45	0.47	0.04	0.24	1.00	0.50	0.29
REITs	0.10	0.77	0.69	0.25	0.51	0.56	0.58	0.64	0.55	0.06	0.21	0.50	1.00	0.35
Commodities	0.01	0.38	0.44	0.12	0.39	0.26	0.35	0.32	0.38	0.06	0.22	0.29	0.35	1.00

Appendix– 5: Covariance and correlation matrices including microfinance (quantitative approach)

	MM USD	EQ World	EQ EM	FI World	FI IL	FI EM	FI CRE	FI HY	FI CB	FI CAT	HF	PE	REITs	COM	FI MF
Money Market USD	0.0000	0.0000	0.0000	-0.0001	0.0000	0.0000	0.0000	0.0000	0.0000	0.0000	0.0001	0.0002	0.0000	0.0001	0.0000
Equities World	0.0000	0.0323	0.0398	0.0020	0.0063	0.0115	0.0078	0.0149	0.0195	0.0012	0.0073	0.0384	0.0310	0.0181	-0.0001
Equities EM	0.0000	0.0398	0.0659	0.0016	0.0080	0.0176	0.0107	0.0218	0.0269	0.0017	0.0117	0.0542	0.0395	0.0299	-0.0002
Gov Bonds World	0.0000	0.0020	0.0016	0.0049	0.0043	0.0022	0.0037	0.0013	0.0025	0.0003	0.0005	-0.0024	0.0040	0.0023	0.0000
Gov Bonds Inflation Linked	-0.0001	0.0063	0.0080	0.0043	0.0076	0.0044	0.0057	0.0047	0.0056	0.0007	0.0020	0.0038	0.0098	0.0089	0.0000
Gov Bonds EM	0.0000	0.0115	0.0176	0.0022	0.0044	0.0121	0.0055	0.0096	0.0093	0.0008	0.0037	0.0156	0.0137	0.0076	0.0000
Credit Bonds	0.0000	0.0078	0.0107	0.0037	0.0057	0.0055	0.0082	0.0069	0.0072	0.0008	0.0026	0.0078	0.0118	0.0085	0.0000
High Yield Bonds	0.0000	0.0149	0.0218	0.0013	0.0047	0.0096	0.0069	0.0166	0.0115	0.0013	0.0047	0.0208	0.0183	0.0110	0.0000
Convertible Bonds	0.0000	0.0195	0.0269	0.0025	0.0056	0.0093	0.0072	0.0115	0.0213	0.0013	0.0070	0.0250	0.0178	0.0148	-0.0001
Cat Bonds	0.0000	0.0012	0.0017	0.0003	0.0007	0.0008	0.0008	0.0013	0.0013	0.0151	0.0007	0.0019	0.0018	0.0018	0.0000
Hedge Funds	0.0000	0.0073	0.0117	0.0005	0.0020	0.0037	0.0026	0.0047	0.0070	0.0007	0.0200	0.0121	0.0065	0.0082	-0.0001
Private Equity	0.0001	0.0384	0.0542	-0.0024	0.0038	0.0156	0.0078	0.0208	0.0250	0.0019	0.0121	0.1307	0.0408	0.0275	-0.0003
REITs	0.0002	0.0310	0.0395	0.0040	0.0098	0.0137	0.0118	0.0183	0.0178	0.0018	0.0065	0.0408	0.0500	0.0207	0.0001
Commodities	0.0000	0.0181	0.0299	0.0023	0.0089	0.0076	0.0085	0.0110	0.0148	0.0018	0.0082	0.0275	0.0207	0.0708	-0.0005
Credit - Microfinance	0.0000	-0.0001	-0.0002	0.0000	0.0000	0.0000	0.0000	0.0000	-0.0001	0.0000	-0.0001	-0.0003	0.0001	-0.0005	0.0073
Risk	**0.5%**	**18.0%**	**25.7%**	**7.0%**	**8.7%**	**11.0%**	**9.1%**	**12.9%**	**14.6%**	**12.3%**	**14.1%**	**36.2%**	**22.4%**	**26.6%**	**8.5%**

	MM USD	EQ World	EQ EM	FI World	FI IL	FI EM	FI CRE	FI HY	FI CB	FI CAT	HF	PE	REITs	COM	FI MF
Money Market USD	1.00	0.01	-0.01	-0.08	-0.04	0.00	-0.04	-0.04	0.00	0.01	0.04	0.06	0.02	0.05	0.02
Equities World	0.01	1.00	0.86	0.16	0.40	0.58	0.48	0.64	0.75	0.06	0.29	0.59	0.77	0.38	0.00
Equities EM	0.01	0.86	1.00	0.09	0.36	0.62	0.46	0.66	0.72	0.05	0.32	0.58	0.69	0.44	-0.01
Gov Bonds World	-0.03	0.16	0.09	1.00	0.71	0.29	0.58	0.14	0.25	0.03	0.05	-0.09	0.25	0.12	0.00
Gov Bonds Inflation Linked	-0.07	0.40	0.36	0.71	1.00	0.46	0.72	0.41	0.44	0.07	0.16	0.12	0.51	0.39	0.01
Gov Bonds EM	-0.03	0.58	0.62	0.29	0.46	1.00	0.55	0.68	0.58	0.06	0.24	0.39	0.56	0.26	0.00
Credit Bonds	0.00	0.48	0.46	0.58	0.72	0.55	1.00	0.59	0.55	0.07	0.20	0.24	0.58	0.35	0.00
High Yield Bonds	-0.03	0.64	0.66	0.14	0.41	0.68	0.59	1.00	0.61	0.08	0.26	0.45	0.64	0.32	0.00
Convertible Bonds	-0.03	0.75	0.72	0.25	0.44	0.58	0.55	0.61	1.00	0.07	0.34	0.47	0.55	0.38	-0.01
Cat Bonds	0.00	0.06	0.05	0.03	0.07	0.06	0.07	0.08	0.07	1.00	0.04	0.04	0.06	0.06	0.00
Hedge Funds	0.01	0.29	0.32	0.05	0.16	0.24	0.20	0.26	0.34	0.04	1.00	0.24	0.21	0.22	0.00
Private Equity	0.01	0.59	0.58	-0.09	0.12	0.39	0.24	0.45	0.47	0.04	0.24	1.00	0.50	0.29	-0.01
REITs	0.10	0.77	0.69	0.25	0.51	0.56	0.58	0.64	0.55	0.06	0.21	0.50	1.00	0.35	0.01
Commodities	0.01	0.38	0.44	0.12	0.39	0.26	0.35	0.32	0.38	0.06	0.22	0.29	0.35	1.00	-0.02
Credit - Microfinance	0.00	0.00	-0.01	0.00	0.01	0.00	0.00	0.00	-0.01	0.00	0.00	-0.01	0.01	-0.02	1.00

Appendix– 6: Covariance and correlation matrices including microfinance (qualitative approach)

	MM USD	EQ World	EQ EM	FI World	FI IL	FI EM	FI CRE	FI HY	FI CB	FI CAT	HF	PE	REITs	COM	FI MF
Money Market USD	0.0000	0.0000	0.0000	-0.0001	0.0000	0.0000	0.0000	0.0000	0.0000	0.0000	0.0001	0.0002	0.0000	0.0001	0.0001
Equities World	0.0000	0.0323	0.0398	0.0020	0.0063	0.0115	0.0078	0.0149	0.0195	0.0012	0.0073	0.0384	0.0310	0.0181	0.0024
Equities EM	0.0000	0.0398	0.0659	0.0016	0.0080	0.0176	0.0107	0.0218	0.0269	0.0017	0.0117	0.0542	0.0395	0.0299	0.0104
Gov Bonds World	0.0000	0.0020	0.0016	0.0049	0.0043	0.0022	0.0037	0.0013	0.0025	0.0003	0.0005	-0.0024	0.0040	0.0023	0.0019
Gov Bonds Inflation Linked	-0.0001	0.0063	0.0080	0.0043	0.0076	0.0044	0.0057	0.0047	0.0056	0.0007	0.0020	0.0038	0.0098	0.0089	0.0047
Gov Bonds EM	0.0000	0.0115	0.0176	0.0022	0.0044	0.0121	0.0055	0.0096	0.0093	0.0008	0.0037	0.0156	0.0137	0.0076	0.0074
Credit Bonds	0.0000	0.0078	0.0107	0.0037	0.0057	0.0055	0.0082	0.0069	0.0072	0.0008	0.0026	0.0078	0.0118	0.0085	0.0037
High Yield Bonds	0.0000	0.0149	0.0218	0.0013	0.0047	0.0096	0.0069	0.0166	0.0115	0.0013	0.0047	0.0208	0.0183	0.0110	0.0035
Convertible Bonds	0.0000	0.0195	0.0269	0.0025	0.0056	0.0093	0.0072	0.0115	0.0213	0.0013	0.0070	0.0250	0.0178	0.0148	0.0020
Cat Bonds	0.0000	0.0012	0.0017	0.0003	0.0007	0.0008	0.0008	0.0013	0.0013	0.0151	0.0007	0.0019	0.0018	0.0018	0.0033
Hedge Funds	0.0000	0.0073	0.0117	0.0005	0.0020	0.0037	0.0026	0.0047	0.0070	0.0007	0.0200	0.0121	0.0065	0.0082	0.0019
Private Equity	0.0001	0.0384	0.0542	-0.0024	0.0038	0.0156	0.0078	0.0208	0.0250	0.0019	0.0121	0.1307	0.0408	0.0275	0.0049
REITs	0.0002	0.0310	0.0395	0.0040	0.0098	0.0137	0.0118	0.0183	0.0178	0.0018	0.0065	0.0408	0.0500	0.0207	0.0030
Commodities	0.0000	0.0181	0.0299	0.0023	0.0089	0.0076	0.0085	0.0110	0.0148	0.0018	0.0082	0.0275	0.0207	0.0708	0.0000
Credit - Microfinance	0.0000	0.0024	0.0104	0.0019	0.0047	0.0074	0.0037	0.0035	0.0020	0.0033	0.0019	0.0049	0.0030	0.0000	0.0182
Risk	**0.5%**	**18.0%**	**25.7%**	**7.0%**	**8.7%**	**11.0%**	**9.1%**	**12.9%**	**14.6%**	**12.3%**	**14.1%**	**36.2%**	**22.4%**	**26.6%**	**13.5%**

	MM USD	EQ World	EQ EM	FI World	FI IL	FI EM	FI CRE	FI HY	FI CB	FI CAT	HF	PE	REITs	COM	FI MF
Money Market USD	1.00	0.01	-0.01	-0.08	-0.04	0.00	-0.04	-0.04	0.00	0.01	0.04	0.06	0.02	0.05	0.40
Equities World	0.01	1.00	0.86	0.16	0.40	0.58	0.48	0.64	0.75	0.06	0.29	0.59	0.77	0.38	0.20
Equities EM	0.01	0.86	1.00	0.09	0.36	0.62	0.46	0.66	0.72	0.05	0.32	0.58	0.69	0.44	0.40
Gov Bonds World	-0.03	0.16	0.09	1.00	0.71	0.29	0.58	0.14	0.25	0.03	0.05	-0.09	0.25	0.12	0.40
Gov Bonds Inflation Linked	-0.07	0.40	0.36	0.71	1.00	0.46	0.72	0.41	0.44	0.07	0.16	0.12	0.51	0.39	0.60
Gov Bonds EM	-0.03	0.58	0.62	0.29	0.46	1.00	0.55	0.68	0.58	0.06	0.24	0.39	0.56	0.26	0.60
Credit Bonds	0.00	0.48	0.46	0.58	0.72	0.55	1.00	0.59	0.55	0.07	0.20	0.24	0.58	0.35	0.50
High Yield Bonds	-0.03	0.64	0.66	0.14	0.41	0.68	0.59	1.00	0.61	0.08	0.26	0.45	0.64	0.32	0.40
Convertible Bonds	-0.03	0.75	0.72	0.25	0.44	0.58	0.55	0.61	1.00	0.07	0.34	0.47	0.55	0.38	0.30
Cat Bonds	0.00	0.06	0.05	0.03	0.07	0.06	0.07	0.08	0.07	1.00	0.04	0.04	0.06	0.06	0.40
Hedge Funds	0.01	0.29	0.32	0.05	0.16	0.24	0.20	0.26	0.34	0.04	1.00	0.24	0.21	0.22	0.30
Private Equity	0.01	0.59	0.58	-0.09	0.12	0.39	0.24	0.45	0.47	0.04	0.24	1.00	0.50	0.29	0.20
REITs	0.10	0.77	0.69	0.25	0.51	0.56	0.58	0.64	0.55	0.06	0.21	0.50	1.00	0.35	0.30
Commodities	0.01	0.38	0.44	0.12	0.39	0.26	0.35	0.32	0.38	0.06	0.22	0.29	0.35	1.00	0.10
Credit - Microfinance	0.40	0.20	0.40	0.40	0.60	0.60	0.50	0.40	0.30	0.40	0.30	0.20	0.30	0.10	1.00

Appendix– 7: Optimized portfolio weights excluding microfinance

	lambda											
	0.5	0.75	1	1.25	1.5	2	2.5	3.25	4	5	7	10
Money Market USD	0.0%	0.0%	0.0%	0.0%	0.0%	0.0%	0.0%	20.0%	20.0%	20.0%	20.0%	20.0%
Equities World	0.0%	0.0%	3.4%	6.7%	8.2%	7.7%	7.1%	5.5%	5.1%	4.7%	4.0%	3.1%
Equities EM	81.1%	64.3%	44.5%	31.9%	24.5%	16.5%	12.1%	9.2%	6.7%	4.5%	1.7%	0.0%
Gov Bonds World	0.0%	0.0%	0.0%	0.0%	0.0%	11.1%	20.7%	17.9%	23.4%	28.3%	34.2%	38.9%
Gov Bonds Inflation Linked	0.0%	0.0%	0.0%	0.0%	0.0%	0.0%	0.0%	0.0%	0.0%	0.0%	0.0%	0.0%
Gov Bonds EM	0.0%	0.0%	0.0%	0.0%	0.0%	0.0%	0.0%	0.0%	0.0%	0.0%	0.0%	0.0%
Credit Bonds	0.0%	0.0%	0.0%	0.1%	9.2%	11.5%	10.6%	8.3%	7.8%	6.8%	4.2%	2.2%
High Yield Bonds	0.0%	0.0%	0.0%	0.0%	0.0%	0.0%	0.0%	0.0%	0.0%	0.8%	3.9%	6.2%
Convertible Bonds	0.0%	1.7%	8.4%	11.7%	10.2%	7.8%	6.2%	4.9%	3.9%	3.1%	1.8%	0.8%
Cat Bonds	0.0%	5.3%	15.0%	20.6%	21.8%	21.7%	21.2%	16.8%	16.6%	16.2%	15.7%	15.3%
Hedge Funds	0.0%	14.5%	18.0%	20.1%	19.7%	18.4%	17.3%	13.7%	13.1%	12.5%	11.7%	11.1%
Private Equity	18.9%	14.1%	10.2%	7.7%	6.5%	5.3%	4.8%	3.7%	3.4%	3.1%	2.7%	2.4%
REITs	0.0%	0.0%	0.5%	1.2%	0.0%	0.0%	0.0%	0.0%	0.0%	0.0%	0.0%	0.0%
Commodities	0.0%	0.0%	0.0%	0.0%	0.0%	0.0%	0.0%	0.0%	0.0%	0.0%	0.0%	0.0%
Return p.a.	**11.59%**	**10.22%**	**8.85%**	**8.02%**	**7.37%**	**6.47%**	**5.90%**	**5.05%**	**4.73%**	**4.44%**	**4.09%**	**3.83%**
Risk p.a.	**25.42%**	**20.93%**	**16.66%**	**14.24%**	**12.45%**	**10.13%**	**8.79%**	**6.87%**	**6.18%**	**5.63%**	**5.07%**	**4.76%**
Shortfall in years	**13.00**	**11.33**	**9.59**	**8.53**	**7.72**	**6.64**	**6.00**	**5.01**	**4.63**	**4.36**	**4.16**	**4.16**

Appendix– 8: Optimized portfolio weights including microfinance (quantitative approach) – risk factor set to 8.5%

	lambda											
	0.5	**0.75**	**1**	**1.25**	**1.5**	**2**	**2.5**	**3.25**	**4**	**5**	**7**	**10**
Money Market USD	0.0%	0.0%	0.0%	0.0%	0.0%	0.0%	0.0%	0.0%	0.0%	13.5%	20.0%	20.0%
Equities World	0.0%	0.0%	0.0%	0.0%	0.0%	2.0%	3.5%	3.9%	3.6%	3.0%	2.6%	2.2%
Equities EM	81.1%	61.9%	47.9%	38.9%	31.8%	22.0%	15.9%	10.8%	8.1%	6.3%	3.9%	1.7%
Gov Bonds World	0.0%	0.0%	0.0%	0.0%	0.0%	0.0%	0.0%	3.5%	10.4%	11.1%	15.5%	21.1%
Gov Bonds Inflation Linked	0.0%	0.0%	0.0%	0.0%	0.0%	0.0%	0.0%	0.0%	0.0%	0.0%	0.0%	0.0%
Gov Bonds EM	0.0%	0.0%	0.0%	0.0%	0.0%	0.0%	0.0%	0.0%	0.0%	0.0%	0.0%	0.0%
Credit Bonds	0.0%	0.0%	0.0%	0.0%	0.0%	0.0%	2.2%	6.7%	6.4%	5.4%	4.7%	3.2%
High Yield Bonds	0.0%	0.0%	0.0%	0.0%	0.0%	0.0%	0.0%	0.0%	0.0%	0.0%	0.0%	1.9%
Convertible Bonds	0.0%	0.0%	0.0%	0.0%	2.6%	5.6%	6.3%	5.2%	4.3%	3.5%	2.6%	1.7%
Cat Bonds	0.0%	0.0%	0.0%	1.2%	4.8%	9.1%	11.4%	12.3%	12.5%	10.8%	10.2%	10.2%
Hedge Funds	0.0%	0.0%	3.7%	7.5%	8.6%	10.0%	10.7%	10.6%	10.3%	8.8%	7.9%	7.6%
Private Equity	18.9%	13.8%	10.6%	8.5%	7.1%	5.1%	4.0%	3.2%	2.9%	2.5%	2.1%	1.8%
REITs	0.0%	0.0%	0.0%	0.0%	0.0%	0.0%	0.0%	0.0%	0.0%	0.0%	0.0%	0.0%
Commodities	0.0%	0.0%	0.0%	0.0%	0.0%	0.0%	0.0%	0.0%	0.0%	0.0%	0.0%	0.0%
Microfinance debt	0.0%	24.2%	37.8%	43.9%	45.0%	46.2%	46.1%	43.8%	41.4%	35.0%	30.6%	28.6%
Return p.a.	**11.59%**	**9.87%**	**8.68%**	**7.93%**	**7.39%**	**6.70%**	**6.26%**	**5.77%**	**5.42%**	**4.86%**	**4.39%**	**4.12%**
Risk p.a.	**25.42%**	**19.34%**	**15.33%**	**12.96%**	**11.31%**	**9.36%**	**8.24%**	**7.13%**	**6.41%**	**5.36%**	**4.52%**	**4.13%**
Shortfall in years	**13.00**	**10.38**	**8.44**	**7.22**	**6.34**	**5.28**	**4.69**	**4.13**	**3.78**	**3.29**	**2.86**	**2.73**

Appendix– 9: Optimized portfolio weights including microfinance (qualitative approach) – risk factor set to 13.5%

	lambda											
	0.5	0.75	1	1.25	1.5	2	2.5	3.25	4	5	7	10
Money Market USD	0.0%	0.0%	0.0%	0.0%	0.0%	0.0%	0.0%	20.0%	20.0%	20.0%	20.0%	20.0%
Equities World	0.0%	0.0%	3.4%	6.7%	8.2%	7.9%	8.2%	6.3%	6.5%	6.6%	5.8%	3.4%
Equities EM	81.1%	64.3%	44.5%	32.0%	24.4%	16.3%	11.1%	8.3%	5.4%	2.7%	0.0%	0.0%
Gov Bonds World	0.0%	0.0%	0.0%	0.0%	0.0%	10.9%	19.4%	16.3%	21.8%	26.3%	31.9%	37.5%
Gov Bonds Inflation Linked	0.0%	0.0%	0.0%	0.0%	0.0%	0.0%	0.0%	0.0%	0.0%	0.0%	0.0%	0.0%
Gov Bonds EM	0.0%	0.0%	0.0%	0.0%	0.0%	0.0%	0.0%	0.0%	0.0%	0.0%	0.0%	0.0%
Credit Bonds	0.0%	0.0%	0.0%	0.0%	9.2%	11.1%	9.7%	8.2%	6.6%	5.5%	2.5%	0.5%
High Yield Bonds	0.0%	0.0%	0.0%	0.0%	0.0%	0.0%	0.0%	0.0%	0.0%	0.5%	3.6%	5.6%
Convertible Bonds	0.0%	1.7%	8.4%	11.7%	10.2%	8.0%	6.8%	5.5%	4.7%	4.0%	2.9%	1.5%
Cat Bonds	0.0%	5.3%	15.0%	20.7%	21.8%	21.5%	20.5%	16.3%	15.7%	15.2%	14.4%	14.2%
Hedge Funds	0.0%	14.5%	18.0%	20.1%	19.7%	18.4%	17.2%	13.6%	12.9%	12.3%	11.4%	10.7%
Private Equity	18.9%	14.1%	10.2%	7.7%	6.5%	5.3%	4.7%	3.7%	3.3%	3.0%	2.6%	2.2%
REITs	0.0%	0.0%	0.6%	1.1%	0.0%	0.0%	0.0%	0.0%	0.0%	0.0%	0.0%	0.0%
Commodities	0.0%	0.0%	0.0%	0.0%	0.0%	0.0%	0.0%	0.0%	0.0%	0.0%	0.0%	0.0%
Microfinance debt	0.0%	0.0%	0.0%	0.0%	0.0%	0.6%	2.5%	1.9%	3.1%	3.9%	4.8%	4.5%
Return p.a.	**11.59%**	**10.22%**	**8.85%**	**8.02%**	**7.37%**	**6.46%**	**5.89%**	**5.04%**	**4.71%**	**4.42%**	**4.07%**	**3.84%**
Risk p.a.	**25.42%**	**20.93%**	**16.66%**	**14.24%**	**12.45%**	**10.12%**	**8.76%**	**6.86%**	**6.14%**	**5.58%**	**5.02%**	**4.73%**
Shortfall in years	**13.00**	**11.33**	**9.59**	**8.53**	**7.72**	**6.64**	**5.98**	**5.00**	**4.59**	**4.31**	**4.11**	**4.10**

Appendix– 10: Optimized portfolio weights including microfinance with risk factor set to 10%

	lambda											
	0.5	**0.75**	**1**	**1.25**	**1.5**	**2**	**2.5**	**3.25**	**4**	**5**	**7**	**10**
Money Market USD	0.0%	0.0%	0.0%	0.0%	0.0%	0.0%	0.0%	12.6%	20.0%	20.0%	20.0%	20.0%
Equities World	0.0%	0.0%	3.4%	6.9%	10.1%	12.4%	12.3%	10.6%	9.6%	9.5%	6.3%	3.8%
Equities EM	81.1%	64.3%	44.5%	31.5%	22.2%	12.0%	7.2%	4.3%	2.4%	0.0%	0.0%	0.0%
Gov Bonds World	0.0%	0.0%	0.0%	0.0%	0.0%	3.4%	12.1%	14.4%	16.0%	20.3%	27.8%	32.7%
Gov Bonds Inflation Linked	0.0%	0.0%	0.0%	0.0%	0.0%	0.0%	0.0%	0.0%	0.0%	0.0%	0.0%	0.0%
Gov Bonds EM	0.0%	0.0%	0.0%	0.0%	0.0%	0.0%	0.0%	0.0%	0.0%	0.0%	0.0%	0.0%
Credit Bonds	0.0%	0.0%	0.0%	0.0%	2.5%	7.3%	5.9%	4.6%	3.8%	3.2%	0.6%	0.0%
High Yield Bonds	0.0%	0.0%	0.0%	0.0%	0.0%	0.0%	0.0%	0.0%	0.0%	0.0%	2.4%	4.0%
Convertible Bonds	0.0%	1.7%	8.4%	11.5%	11.6%	10.3%	9.0%	7.3%	6.3%	5.7%	3.8%	2.2%
Cat Bonds	0.0%	5.3%	15.0%	19.2%	18.9%	18.0%	17.1%	14.6%	13.1%	12.6%	12.4%	12.3%
Hedge Funds	0.0%	14.5%	18.0%	19.4%	18.6%	17.2%	16.0%	13.4%	11.9%	11.3%	10.5%	9.9%
Private Equity	18.9%	14.1%	10.2%	7.8%	6.4%	5.0%	4.4%	3.6%	3.1%	2.8%	2.3%	1.9%
REITs	0.0%	0.0%	0.6%	1.1%	0.7%	0.0%	0.0%	0.0%	0.0%	0.0%	0.0%	0.0%
Commodities	0.0%	0.0%	0.0%	0.0%	0.0%	0.0%	0.0%	0.0%	0.0%	0.0%	0.0%	0.0%
Microfinance debt	0.0%	0.0%	0.0%	2.7%	9.0%	14.4%	16.0%	14.5%	13.8%	14.6%	13.9%	13.2%
Return p.a.	**11.6%**	**10.2%**	**8.8%**	**8.0%**	**7.3%**	**6.4%**	**5.9%**	**5.1%**	**4.7%**	**4.4%**	**4.1%**	**3.9%**
Risk p.a.	**25.4%**	**20.9%**	**16.7%**	**14.2%**	**12.4%**	**10.2%**	**8.8%**	**7.2%**	**6.2%**	**5.7%**	**5.2%**	**4.9%**
Shortfall in years	**13.00**	**11.33**	**9.59**	**8.51**	**7.75**	**6.76**	**6.14**	**5.32**	**4.76**	**4.51**	**4.33**	**4.31**

Appendix– 11: Optimized portfolio weights including microfinance with risk factor set to 12%

	lambda											
	0.5	**0.75**	**1**	**1.25**	**1.5**	**2**	**2.5**	**3.25**	**4**	**5**	**7**	**10**
Money Market USD	0.0%	0.0%	0.0%	0.0%	0.0%	0.0%	0.0%	18.1%	20.0%	20.0%	20.0%	20.0%
Equities World	0.0%	0.0%	3.4%	6.6%	8.5%	9.7%	9.8%	7.9%	7.8%	7.7%	6.0%	3.5%
Equities EM	81.1%	64.3%	44.5%	31.9%	24.2%	14.6%	9.5%	6.9%	4.2%	1.7%	0.0%	0.0%
Gov Bonds World	0.0%	0.0%	0.0%	0.0%	0.0%	8.6%	17.1%	15.9%	20.0%	24.3%	30.7%	36.2%
Gov Bonds Inflation Linked	0.0%	0.0%	0.0%	0.0%	0.0%	0.0%	0.0%	0.0%	0.0%	0.0%	0.0%	0.0%
Gov Bonds EM	0.0%	0.0%	0.0%	0.0%	0.0%	0.0%	0.0%	0.0%	0.0%	0.0%	0.0%	0.0%
Credit Bonds	0.0%	0.0%	0.0%	0.0%	8.6%	9.7%	8.3%	6.5%	5.6%	4.6%	1.8%	0.0%
High Yield Bonds	0.0%	0.0%	0.0%	0.0%	0.0%	0.0%	0.0%	0.0%	0.0%	0.3%	3.2%	5.1%
Convertible Bonds	0.0%	1.7%	8.4%	11.8%	10.3%	8.8%	7.6%	6.0%	5.3%	4.7%	3.2%	1.8%
Cat Bonds	0.0%	5.3%	15.0%	20.7%	21.5%	20.3%	19.4%	15.7%	14.8%	14.3%	13.7%	13.6%
Hedge Funds	0.0%	14.5%	18.0%	20.1%	19.6%	18.0%	16.8%	13.5%	12.6%	12.0%	11.1%	10.5%
Private Equity	18.9%	14.1%	10.2%	7.7%	6.5%	5.2%	4.6%	3.6%	3.2%	2.9%	2.5%	2.1%
REITs	0.0%	0.0%	0.5%	1.2%	0.0%	0.0%	0.0%	0.0%	0.0%	0.0%	0.0%	0.0%
Commodities	0.0%	0.0%	0.0%	0.0%	0.0%	0.0%	0.0%	0.0%	0.0%	0.0%	0.0%	0.0%
Microfinance debt	0.0%	0.0%	0.0%	0.0%	0.8%	5.0%	6.8%	5.8%	6.6%	7.5%	7.7%	7.3%
Return p.a.	**11.6%**	**10.2%**	**8.8%**	**8.0%**	**7.4%**	**6.4%**	**5.9%**	**5.1%**	**4.7%**	**4.4%**	**4.1%**	**3.9%**
Risk p.a.	**25.4%**	**20.9%**	**16.7%**	**14.2%**	**12.4%**	**10.1%**	**8.7%**	**6.9%**	**6.1%**	**5.6%**	**5.0%**	**4.8%**
Shortfall in years	**13.00**	**11.33**	**9.59**	**8.53**	**7.72**	**6.63**	**5.99**	**5.04**	**4.60**	**4.33**	**4.13**	**4.12**

Appendix– 12: Optimized portfolio weights including microfinance with risk factor set to 15%

	lambda											
	0.5	**0.75**	**1**	**1.25**	**1.5**	**2**	**2.5**	**3.25**	**4**	**5**	**7**	**10**
Money Market USD	0.0%	0.0%	0.0%	0.0%	0.0%	0.0%	0.0%	20.0%	20.0%	20.0%	20.0%	20.0%
Equities World	0.0%	0.0%	3.4%	6.6%	8.2%	7.7%	7.1%	5.5%	5.5%	5.5%	5.3%	3.3%
Equities EM	81.1%	64.3%	44.5%	32.0%	24.4%	16.5%	12.1%	9.2%	6.4%	3.7%	0.4%	0.0%
Gov Bonds World	0.0%	0.0%	0.0%	0.0%	0.0%	11.1%	20.7%	17.9%	23.0%	27.5%	32.9%	38.2%
Gov Bonds Inflation Linked	0.0%	0.0%	0.0%	0.0%	0.0%	0.0%	0.0%	0.0%	0.0%	0.0%	0.0%	0.0%
Gov Bonds EM	0.0%	0.0%	0.0%	0.0%	0.0%	0.0%	0.0%	0.0%	0.0%	0.0%	0.0%	0.0%
Credit Bonds	0.0%	0.0%	0.0%	0.0%	9.3%	11.5%	10.6%	8.3%	7.5%	6.2%	3.2%	1.1%
High Yield Bonds	0.0%	0.0%	0.0%	0.0%	0.0%	0.0%	0.0%	0.0%	0.0%	0.7%	3.8%	5.9%
Convertible Bonds	0.0%	1.7%	8.4%	11.8%	10.2%	7.8%	6.2%	4.9%	4.1%	3.5%	2.5%	1.2%
Cat Bonds	0.0%	5.3%	15.0%	20.7%	21.8%	21.7%	21.2%	16.9%	16.4%	15.8%	15.0%	14.7%
Hedge Funds	0.0%	14.5%	18.0%	20.1%	19.7%	18.4%	17.3%	13.7%	13.0%	12.4%	11.6%	10.9%
Private Equity	18.9%	14.1%	10.2%	7.7%	6.5%	5.3%	4.8%	3.7%	3.4%	3.1%	2.6%	2.2%
REITs	0.0%	0.0%	0.6%	1.2%	0.0%	0.0%	0.0%	0.0%	0.0%	0.0%	0.0%	0.0%
Commodities	0.0%	0.0%	0.0%	0.0%	0.0%	0.0%	0.0%	0.0%	0.0%	0.0%	0.0%	0.0%
Microfinance debt	0.0%	0.0%	0.0%	0.0%	0.0%	0.0%	0.0%	0.0%	0.7%	1.6%	2.6%	2.5%
Return p.a.	**11.6%**	**10.2%**	**8.8%**	**8.0%**	**7.4%**	**6.5%**	**5.9%**	**5.1%**	**4.7%**	**4.4%**	**4.1%**	**3.8%**
Risk p.a.	**25.4%**	**20.9%**	**16.7%**	**14.2%**	**12.4%**	**10.1%**	**8.8%**	**6.9%**	**6.2%**	**5.6%**	**5.0%**	**4.7%**
Shortfall in years	**13.00**	**11.33**	**9.59**	**8.53**	**7.72**	**6.64**	**6.00**	**5.01**	**4.62**	**4.33**	**4.12**	**4.12**

MIX
Papier aus verantwortungsvollen Quellen
Paper from responsible sources
FSC® C105338

If you have any concerns about our products,
you can contact us on
ProductSafety@springernature.com

In case Publisher is established outside the EU,
the EU authorized representative is:
Springer Nature Customer Service Center GmbH
Europaplatz 3, 69115 Heidelberg, Germany

Printed by Libri Plureos GmbH
in Hamburg, Germany